GUERRILLA BIBLE STUDIES

VOLUME 4

FOLLOWING JESUS: ON EARTH AS IN HEAVEN

BOB EKBLAD

THE PEOPLE'S SEMINARY PRESS

GUERRILLA BIBLE STUDIES
Volume 4
Following Jesus: On Earth As In Heaven

The People's Seminary Press
P.O. BOX 410
Burlington, WA 98233
www.peoplesseminary.org

ISBN: 978-1-954387-05-8

Made in the USA.

PREFACE

Jesus of Nazareth is my inspiration for life and ministry and for what I like to call "guerrilla Bible studies." The life and teaching of Jesus, as recorded in the Gospels of the New Testament, embody the word gospel, which means "good news" or "liberating message." According to New Testament Scriptures, Jesus is God's Son, Israel's Messiah, and the Lord himself in the flesh. He was born into a world marked by oppression and injustice to announce and embody God's global liberation movement. I use the term guerrilla Bible studies to alert readers to the way that Jesus launched a movement from inside the established order, which radically challenged the status quo, and also to link these studies with my book *Guerrilla Gospel: Reading the Bible for Liberation in the Power of the Spirit.*[1] Jesus came to bring liberating change, both from below and from above—in that he came "from above!" He came to minister from the margins inward, serving the ordinary people of his day from Galilee and Samaria to Jerusalem.

Like an insurgent, Jesus comes in under the radar, behind enemy lines, establishing a foundation of trust with a growing entourage of humble followers. He challenges the authorities of his day, along with their legal systems, and he calls others to join him. He incites a revolution, which he calls the Kingdom of God. He starts out incognito, but after his baptism at age thirty, he goes public. He teaches and ministers with unprecedented authority, which is backed up by acts of healing, advocacy, and liberation on behalf of the oppressed, poor, and disenfranchised. In Jesus' many encounters in the Gospels, he breaks the established rules to advocate for the marginalized. He confronts the powers—both visible and invisible— and models a holistic spiritual warfare that brings freedom.

Jesus met and called ordinary people to follow him, to become his disciples. He calls you, me, and everyone, to join him in announcing the good news of God's coming kingdom on earth as in heaven.

I am compelled by the way Jesus loves people so freely and effectively wherever he goes, seeking and finding the lost and forsaken, raising up the

1. Bob Ekblad, *Guerrilla Gospel: Reading the Bible for Liberation in the Power of the Spirit* (Burlington: The People's Seminary Press, 2018).

downtrodden and hopeless, offering abundant life to all who will follow him. Reading about Jesus in the Gospels inspires me to follow him, go deep with him, tune into his instructions for my daily life, and work with him to reach others with the good news he embodies and proclaims throughout the New Testament. Studying Jesus' life and teaching also helps us identify the presence of this same God in the Old Testament stories.

I've written *Guerrilla Bible Studies* fifteen years after *Reading the Bible with the Damned*, my first attempt to communicate a liberating way of reading the Bible. The studies in this volume are designed to be concrete guides for Bible study facilitators or individuals doing their own personal study. The third volume, *Basic Training for the Jesus Movement*, follows volume 1 *Surprising Encounters with God*, and volume 2, *God's Radical Recruiting*, providing thirteen Bible studies on Jesus' core teaching on what it means to be a fully-engaged disciple.

The *Guerrilla Bible Studies* companion series is designed for people who are discerning their callings as disciples of Jesus, desire further training, and want to embark on the adventurous journey of facilitating liberating Bible studies. When we look at how Jesus engaged people during his earthly ministry, we see him moving in freedom, wisdom, and power, combining teaching with signs and wonders that confirmed his words.[2] As you move through these studies, my hope is that you will be personally addressed by the living God, that your ears would be awakened "to listen as a disciple" (Is 50:4), as you are "taught by God" (1 Thes 4:9)—pressing on to maturity (Heb 6:1).

The Bible tells us the story of God's pursuit, liberation, and recruitment of human beings as agents of blessing for the world. God calls people throughout Scripture, launching them as announcers and change agents to bring salvation to the ends of the earth. This fourth volume of *Guerrilla Bible Studies: Following Jesus: On Earth as in Heaven*, is the fourth in a series of four sequels to *Guerrilla Gospel: Reading the Bible for Liberation in the Power of the Spirit*. In this collection you will find practical guidelines for facilitating liberating Bible studies, including a new sample Bible study on Jesus' healing of the man born blind in John 9. These thirteen Bible studies have been tried and tested in jails, rural communities in the global south, frontline North American and European missional settings, and graduate level theology schools. Each study focuses a story involving announcing and embodying the Kingdom of God, inspiring followers of Jesus who are seeking active engagement in his liberation movement. Each study offers facilitators questions and suggestions for guiding the study, explanations and background information about the text, and invitations and calls to action for participants.

2. See my chapter on manifestations of the Spirit that confirm the message in *Guerrilla Gospel*, 129–157.

HOW TO USE THIS GUIDE

Guerrilla Bible studies can be used for personal study or as a guide for leading Bible studies with others. If you plan to go through these studies with others, it is important to go through each Bible study first so that you can find the good news and make the study your own.

The Introduction is a step-by-step guide for facilitating liberating Bible studies, which I have adapted from *Guerrilla Gospel: Reading the Bible for Liberation in the Power of the Spirit.*

Chapters One through Thirteen consist of thirteen Bible studies, which include the passage from Scripture, questions, as well as explanatory notes, background information, and invitational prompts. These studies can be completed in 30 minutes, though 45–60 minutes would be ideal. Facilitators can bring many other questions and insights into these studies, which will depend on the needs of your context and the Spirit's direction.

My preferred version of the Bible in English is the New American Standard Bible, which is a fairly literal translation of the original biblical languages. There are many other versions that can be used in its place. Informed clarifications about language and textual explanations will always be helpful, regardless of which version is used, and this will require preparation on the part of the facilitator.

The collection of Bible studies in this volume is designed to help people receive basic training to advance in their faith and orient their lives as active disciples of Jesus in his liberation movement—the Kingdom of God.

CONTENTS

GLOSSARY OF TERMS

Study Guide	Notes
Introduction	At the beginning of the Bible study, provide a short introduction to the story you are going to read together.
Background	For some texts, it is important to include some background information about what comes before the main story you're discussing in the study.
Read 📖 Invite someone to read the designated passage from the story out loud.	
Explanation ✓	Offer explanations about the text when needed. Don't ask people questions that could make them feel ignorant or that could invite incorrect answers.
Re-read / Optional Reading 📖 In some cases, the study suggests re-reading passages or turning to other Scriptures as part of the discussion.	
Question ? Look around at people as you ask questions. Be gentle and invitational rather than confrontational.	

Study Guide	Notes
Suggestion	Suggestions are occasionally offered to help the Bible study facilitator more effectively guide the conversation.
Invitation ———>	Invitations draw participants together and give them space to share from their own experience or to respond personally to the story in some way.

FACILITATING GUERRILLA BIBLE STUDIES

FACILITATING GUERRILLA BIBLE STUDIES

PREPARING A GUERRILLA BIBLE STUDY

Knowing the people with whom you plan to read the Bible will help you more sensitively and effectively guide them through a biblical text. You can get to know the community where you are ministering by carefully listening to and observing the people. Further study may be necessary to help you understand people's backgrounds and current situations. Following are some general guidelines for becoming an effective guerrilla Bible study facilitator.

Embody God's Love

As facilitators, we are mediators who embody God's tender, unconditional love.[1] Our primary objective is to facilitate an encounter between Jesus and the individuals in our group. We mediate this encounter through the Bible and our own stories and backgrounds. Jesus says that when people receive us, they are receiving him as well as the Father who sent him. Jesus never pressures or manipulates people to follow him, but loves people without strings. Some people may have encountered Christians who don't care about them as individuals, but only about their decisions for salvation. When we demonstrate care for people as individuals, asking them about their lives, responding to their concerns, offering to pray for them and their families, and following up with them when possible, our care builds trust and heals wounds that may have been inflicted by conditional acceptance experienced elsewhere.

Identify Barriers to Relationship

Our unique identities and backgrounds can create many obstacles, depending on the subculture(s) of our reading communities. It's import-

---

1. See Daniel Bourguet, *The Tenderness of God* (Eugene: Cascade Books, 2017).

ant to consider prejudices that people might have about us—or ones they expect us to have about them. These can center around factors such as race, class, national identity, culture, gender, sexual orientation, political party, religion, and denominational affiliation; seek to overcome some of these negative stereotypes.[2]

We each need to rediscover and reaffirm our baptismal identity regularly by dying to the unique distinctions of our flesh, so that our status as God's son or daughter will take precedence in all our engagements with people.[3]

We can lower "us–them" barriers and seek to optimize trust and empowerment with our group by being authentic, humble, and interested in everyone, carrying ourselves in ways that do not reinforce insecurities, especially assumptions about inferiority.

For example, in my work as a jail chaplain, I serve prisoners from a wide range of racial, ethnic, and social class backgrounds. Prisoners may assume that I consider myself superior to them, am in agreement with the state regarding their charges, imprisonment, and sentencing, am a moralistic and judgmental Christian (which may be all they've ever experienced), and represent mainstream white American values. In my efforts to represent Jesus as an ambassador for the Kingdom of God, I often look for ways to differentiate myself naturally so as to challenge people's prejudices and insecurities.

Yet our motivation as facilitators should never be to prove that we are sensitive, politically correct, cross-cultural experts who are worthy of people's trust. The Bible study should not become a place where we seek to vindicate our own unique identities as exceptions to people's prejudices, which will always vary anyway. Nor should we focus too much attention on affirming people's culture, sexual orientation, gang affiliation, social class, or nationality. Rather, our desire should be to focus people's attention on Jesus. We need to minimize barriers so that people can receive God's living word as it is mediated through us—and in spite of us. Trust will naturally grow among us as we humbly point people away from ourselves and towards Jesus, who is the Savior for us all. We can seek to emulate the attitude of John the Baptist towards Jesus when he says, "He must increase, but I must decrease" (Jn 3:30).

2. See Bob Ekblad, "Reading Scripture for Good News Across Barriers of Race/Ethnicity, Class and Culture," *Multicultural Perspectives on Reading the Bible, Interpretation: A Journal of Bible and Theology* 65, no. 3 (July 2011): 229–248.

3. See Bob Ekblad, *A New Christian Manifesto: Pledging Allegiance to the Kingdom of God* (Louisville: Westminster John Knox, 2008), 32–51.

Before Gathering

Prepare spiritually through personal study, prayer, and worship. Spend regular time in God's presence in ways that nourish you, asking the Holy Spirit to fill and refresh you. Ask friends who pray for you to intercede before, during, and after your group Bible studies. Invite the Holy Spirit to give you prophetic revelation about which Scriptures to read, questions to ask, and words of knowledge to offer so that you can engage personally with participants.

Prayerfully decide how you will order your time so that you can accomplish your objectives, taking into consideration time constraints, the makeup of your group, special requests, and other factors. Choose a biblical passage based on these considerations, along with your knowledge of people's needs, their exposure to the Christian faith, and the Spirit's guidance.

Coordinate with your partner or team members, deciding each person's role in advance in order to avoid confusion.

Setting up the Gathering Space

There are unique challenges to facilitating Bible studies, depending on whether you are in someone's home, a shelter, workplace, hospital room, or street corner. Recommended protocols vary greatly from culture to culture, so it will be important to discern what is respectful for your context. Wherever possible, try to find a meeting place where you can safely read Scripture, minister, and where people will feel free to share their thoughts and feelings with minimal interruptions.

Try to set up the space for optimal participation by arranging chairs or couches in a circle whenever possible. A circle places the facilitator at the same level or below those gathered, creating an environment of equality that puts people at ease. If gathering around a table, space chairs so that participants will be comfortable. Try to leave adequate room behind the chairs that would give you room to make your way around the group to pray individually for people if appropriate.

When leading an in-person Bible study during a pandemic, be sure to follow recommended protocols (wearing mask, physical distancing). Standing six feet apart in a circle under a covered area or in the shade of tree is doable. Consider acting out the story in some way. Bible studies can be led through the open window of your vehicle, with others parked close enough apart to hear one another.

Choose a seat or place to stand where everyone can easily see and hear you. If you will be accompanied by others, encourage them to find seats spaced around the circle. This can help minimize "us–them" dynamics, where people's attention is too much on you and your colleagues. In some contexts, people may feel uncomfortable looking at each other and prefer to face the facilitator.

If speaking to a larger group from a lectern, try to move the lectern to the floor in order to minimize the physical distance between you and your audience. If you are being hosted by another leader, sensitively work out these details in advance.

Whenever possible, place a Bible or photocopied sheet with the text on every chair before the study begins. Jails and prisons in North America sometimes only have the King James Version, which can be hard to understand, or highly paraphrased versions that lack sufficient detail. Most languages have translations of the Bible that use vocabulary that is either too difficult for many people or else overly simplified. To avoid these challenges, you may want to bring Bibles or pass out photocopies of the biblical text in the translation you will be using.

If you will be gathering in someone's home, determine a time and space when there will be minimal interruptions. When you arrive, wait to be invited in and be careful not to look around in ways that could bring shame. Accept whatever seating is offered—even the only or best seats. Some people may be ashamed of their living conditions and ask to gather outside. If televisions or radios are playing, let your hosts decide whether or not to turn them off.

BEGINNING A GUERRILLA BIBLE STUDY

Establish Group Rapport

In jails, prisons, or homeless shelters, you might want to stand by the door as people enter, shaking their hands, introducing yourself, and inviting them to take a seat. It's important to establish respectful rapport within the group through introductions. When I introduce myself to a new group, I try to provide them with enough information to establish some basic trust. I often begin by verbally acknowledging apparent differences between myself and the group to establish rapport and set people at ease. With prisoners, I may introduce myself with something like the following.

Hey, you guys, I'm Bob, one of the pastors from Tierra Nueva in Burlington. I've been coming into this jail for over twenty-five years now and consider it a great privilege to be here with you. I am so sorry that you have to be locked up here in the jail right now. Jails and prisons are hard places, and they certainly aren't working to reform people, are they?

You guys each come from backgrounds that are different from each other's—and certainly from mine. Many of you have suffered in ways that I can't even imagine. You see life and will notice things in the Bible that I may never notice. I've never been arrested or jailed, never crossed over the border illegally, never used heroin or meth, and never been in a fight. Though I've been through my own share of suffering, my life's been very different from yours. So I want to hear what you think and if you notice anything that gives you hope as we read the Bible together.

Right at the start, invite participation from everyone in the group by acknowledging that each person brings his or her own unique culture and life perspective, questions, and wisdom. Carefully lay out any necessary ground rules in a gentle, non-legalistic way to provide security for the group. People also appreciate being informed about what you are hoping to accomplish during the time, along with a proposed schedule. Always ask if participants are okay with the plan or if they have other hopes or ideas.

In settings where people already know one another, you might begin with a quick check-in, paying careful attention to how much time you allot to each person so that you can stay within your time limit. In settings where people don't know each other, such as jails, prisons, psychiatric hospitals, or retirement centers, give them clear guidance about what you're asking them to share, such as their first names and where they're from. This humanizes people, especially if they are accustomed to being addressed by their last names or inmate identification numbers.

Use care in making eye contact with people, showing honor and respect according to cultural, gender, and social class considerations. Avoid staring at people, their tattoos, scars, or unique features on their body. In preparation for the study, I sometimes pray, "Jesus, I give you my eyes. May people experience your tender gaze through me. Help me to see each one as you see them." Seek to acknowledge everyone, but avoid showing favoritism or giving too much attention to attention-seeking participants.

Avoid language that over-identifies with people or goes beyond your authentic experience. For example, if you are working with gang-affiliated people but do not come from this background, don't try to gain street credibility by using slang that is not part of your normal vocabulary. Also, avoid using profanity as this can discredit you, create offense, or invite unbridled profanity.

Open with Prayer and Worship

When we begin a Bible study with prayer, we recognize our need for God to help us and we invite the Spirit to open everyone's hearts. When meeting with people who are not from a religious background, I often explain that when we pray, we are talking to God. I always pray with my eyes open, looking gently over everyone who is gathered around the circle.

In rural Honduras, where the groups I used to lead included people who didn't attend church, along with active Roman Catholics, Pentecostals, and Baptists, I learned the importance of beginning gatherings with the Lord's Prayer, or stating that I or another volunteer would give the opening prayer. Without clear instructions, Pentecostals would break out in simultaneous prayer, often in tongues, alarming the rest of the group.

Praying the Lord's Prayer together allowed everyone to participate in an orderly, non-threatening way.

In many settings, it helps to silence or bind voices of accusation or mockery or other spirits you discern right at the beginning, either silently or aloud. We can exercise spiritual authority in alignment with Jesus, who gave his disciples authority to bind and loose spirits (Mt 16:19; 18:18). My opening prayer might include, "In Jesus' name I silence all voices of accusation and mockery, and I welcome the Holy Spirit's presence to bring peace and security." People who are tormented by accusing voices often mention that these voices go dead in response to such declarations—which are not prayers to God but orders directed at predatory invisible realities. I sometimes take time to explain the power of Jesus' name, encouraging people to cry out to Jesus when they feel anxious or tormented.

After the opening prayer, you might consider having a time of singing or silently praying for people around the circle before starting the Bible study. In homeless shelters, jails, and prisons, I tend to avoid having people sing together, since not everyone will know the same songs, and this can create an "us–them" dynamic that gets things off to a bad start. Moreover, songs can also trigger negative or positive nostalgia, which can create unnecessary barriers. People may feel pressured by circumstances or remorse to return to the religion of their upbringing, which may have included toxic elements.

In contexts where singing together is appropriate, choose songs that use accessible language and convey the love of God. If possible, it's also a good idea to have photocopied song sheets available.

In contexts where singing together may not be a good idea, most people are receptive to being prayed for while someone plays guitar and sings a contemplative worship song over them. I always ask people's permission, saying something like, "Before we begin, we'd like to play and sing a worship song. Rather than trying to sing along, we invite you to sit back and receive what God wants to give you to bless and refresh you. During the song, I'd like to pray silently over each of you. If you're not comfortable with me praying for you for whatever reason, no worries. Otherwise, are you okay with me going around and praying for you?" I look around from person to person as I'm speaking to give everyone a chance to express their desire for prayer, or not.

Then I invite the Holy Spirit to bless and comfort us all. I often place my hand gently on each person's shoulder, except when there are no-touch rules, or during a pandemic when social distancing is necessary, when people express reluctance. I always ask people's permission before touching them on the shoulder. As I go around the circle, I sometimes feel led to share a prophetic impression about a possible need for physical or emotional healing or to pray specifically for an individual. Once I've gone around the circle, I ask if people need healing for the conditions I've discerned. Then I pray, inviting people to place their hands wherever they need healing on their body. I always make sure I have people's permission before I minister to them in any way.

Setting the Stage for the Guerrilla Gospel Encounter

I remain open about how to begin the Bible study portion of the gathering based on the Spirit's guidance. Sometimes I give the group options about how to use the remaining time. For example, I might begin with a question or a description of a common problem that people face as a way to get people talking and to prepare them to hear from God through Scripture. In jails, prisons, or other institutional settings, where people have little control over their schedules, I sometimes ask the group if anyone has a pressing question or Scripture they would like to read and discuss. Or I might begin with a story, testimony, or a prophetic impression for healing or personal encouragement. Sometimes I begin by simply reading the biblical text that I've prepared in advance. Another possibility is to begin with a bibliodrama that enacts the story. Bibliodramas draw from the best practices in improv[4] and psychodrama and can powerfully communicate the gospel and make it accessible to different audiences.[5]

4. See Peter Pitzele, *Scripture Windows: Towards a Practice of Bibliodrama* (Los Angeles: Torah Aurora Productions, 1998). For an example of Pitzele's spontaneous bibliodrama, see https://www.youtube.com/watch?v=omvx96XdnXY. You can also watch the introductory sessions on bibliodrama at https://www.youtube.com/watch?v=MNPe0KWlSE0 and https://www.youtube.com/watch?v=-AbrjNwiXDs

5. See Robin Gallaher Branch, *Six Biblical Plays for Contemporary Audiences* (Eugene: Cascade Books, 2016).

Spontaneously gathering volunteers to act out a biblical story can also get people's attention in fresh ways, particularly when combined with a text-based Bible study. I often put together simple bibliodramas, such as Jesus' calling of Simon through the miraculous catch (Lk 5:1–11), the healing of the woman bent over double (Lk 13:10–17),[6] Jesus' encounter with the woman caught in adultery (Jn 4),[7] and the healing of the man who was lame from birth (Acts 3:1–10). To put together a spontaneous bibliodrama, you need to know the biblical story well, be able to think quickly on your feet as you facilitate, and have someone read the story clearly and loudly so that everyone can hear the Scripture as it's being performed.

GUIDING PARTICIPANTS INTO THE GUERRILLA GOSPEL ENCOUNTER

The Bible contains the larger story of God's liberation movement.[8] Within this overarching biblical narrative, there are many smaller stories that are situated in unique settings. Some stories or teachings will appear more immediately relevant to you and your group than others. As you turn to the biblical text, begin by providing a short but compelling explanation about why you're inviting people to look at this particular passage. This will help participants feel secure and engaged from the start. Also, some people may want to understand why you are reading something from the middle or end of the Bible rather than starting at the beginning, as you would any other book.

Next, briefly outline God's mission in the world in a way that will connect personally with the background and composition of your group. Be sure to use clear, simple language rather than religious jargon or complicated theological vocabulary. When considering how to summarize the Bible to prepare for a particular text, it is wise to determine the key points in advance.

Before turning to an example of what this summary introduction might look like for Philippians 4:4-9, there are some important things to keep in mind as you help your group navigate the Bible. Remember that for some participants, the biblical narrative might be new or hostile territory.

---

6. See Bob Ekblad, *The Beautiful Gate: Enter Jesus' Global Liberation Movement* (Burlington: The People's Seminary Press, 2017), 76–79.

7. See Ekblad, "Reading Scripture for Good News," 243–249.

8. See Ekblad, *Guerrilla Gospel*, 21–36.

Navigation Tips

First, in order to keep everyone focused, it's a good idea to divide the biblical narrative into pre-determined sections that are no more than one to three verses long.[9] When you read more than three verses of Scripture aloud, people are likely to become distracted and miss some critical content, especially if you are reading in more than one language.

Another objective in reading shorter sections of Scripture is to slow down the reading process, which invites contemplation. At the same time, be aware of time limitations, people's attention spans, and their level of engagement so that you can keep the momentum going and hold people's interest. Holding people's attention is a critical aspect of setting the stage for the unfolding biblical narrative.

Second, people who are unfamiliar with the Bible may feel intimidated or embarrassed when they cannot readily find the biblical passage, so show people where to find the passage in the Bible by providing photocopies or a page number if possible. Give people enough time to locate the passage. If people have different versions of the Bible with different page numbers and you see them struggling, gently help individuals find the text. I often try to diffuse any shame from the start by stating that there are many different books in the Bible, and many of them are short and quite difficult to find.

Third, I also try to diffuse shame at the beginning of a Bible study by acknowledging that the Bible is foreign and has many words, names, and places that are difficult to pronounce. If a reader has limited reading ability, offer gentle encouragement and help with difficult pronunciation, but don't bother with pronunciation that makes no difference to the meaning (like names of people and places). Also, the biblical text can spring to life in fresh ways when read slowly or haltingly by an amateur reader.

Fourth, if the same person continually volunteers to read, suggest that someone who hasn't read yet read the next verses or re-read a text that needs closer study. Never pressure anyone to read aloud or offer their opinions.

Fifth, try to ask questions that anyone in the group could answer. I would never ask who the Pharisees or Sadducees are, what a parable is, or why Jewish religious leaders didn't think Jesus should heal on the Sabbath. Questions that require background knowledge can cause people to feel potentially stupid or ashamed, or require you to publicly correct someone who gives an incorrect answer. I find it best to offer the most

9. See Ekblad, *Guerrilla Gospel*, 93–106.

essential definitions myself and then to ask questions that people can answer in the biblical passage we've just read. If I see people hesitating, I often invite someone to re-read the verse we're discussing, and then I ask the question again. If a question doesn't bear fruit, I abandon it and try another. Questions should move the conversation along and help people determine the meaning of the text as they read it in direct rapport with their lives.

Sixth, you may consider dividing a larger group into small groups to discuss the verses, questions, contemporary equivalents, or possible responses. Small group discussions work well with students, church groups, or people who are accustomed to working together. Identifying or assigning small group facilitators can help keep the group on track and assure that everyone has an opportunity to speak. If your group is made up of inmates, people with mental health issues, or those who are under the influence of drugs or alcohol, small group facilitators must be especially skilled. If skilled small group facilitators are not available, it is best to keep the larger group together.

Seventh, it can be helpful to record people's responses to questions on large pads of paper or a white board when possible, as people often feel empowered when they see their answers written down. However, facilitators will need to develop the ability to summarize and record people's responses accurately, spell sufficiently, and write legibly.

Eighth, if you are working with a mixed group (including people from diverse denominations), you may need to use biblical versions that are considered sacred by each group. If your Bible study is bilingual or trilingual, it is important to have the Scripture read out loud in each of the languages represented within the group or to have interpreter(s) offer simultaneous translations. If there are a small number of people from a different language group and time is limited, you might suggest that these individuals read along silently in their own language, though simultaneous interpretation would be better. This is particularly important for groups with participants who are illiterate or don't have reading glasses (which is common in a jail or prison context).

Finally, if you are using an interpreter, be attentive to the interpreter's skill level and adjust the speed of your delivery as necessary. Model respectful partnership by occasionally confirming that both the people and the interpreter are understanding. Pay attention to those on the margins of the group and try to include them. At the break, check with a couple of fluent bilingual people in the group to make sure the interpreter is accurate. If not, you might find a backup interpreter to take over to give the first interpreter a break.

JOURNEYING THROUGH A GUERRILLA GOSPEL ENCOUNTER

The healing of the man born blind in John 9:1-41 has become especially real and highly relevant to our Tierra Nueva community. This story fits well into this volume of missional Bible studies, *Following Jesus: On Earth as in Heaven.* Though Jesus here heals a man born blind, he simultaneously empowers this man (and others who identify with him) as a prophetic voice, sending him to challenge religious excluders then and now.

Sample Introduction – longer (John 9)

The Gospel of John is the fourth book in the New Testament that presents Jesus' life and teaching. In John 1-8 many teachings and actions of Jesus prepare us to better understand the story of the healing of the man blind from birth in John 9.

Right from the start John identifies the word as creating the world, as being with God, as being God himself, life and light that shines in the darkness. Though the word is coming into the world to enlighten all people, the word is not recognized by the world, nor received by God's people (Jn 1:9-11). This rejection culminates in Jesus' death by execution, as tensions mount from story to story as John's Gospel progresses. Those who do receive are themselves given authority to become children of God. This word becomes flesh in Jesus. When Jesus speaks, his word mobilizes, heals, and transforms. Look for how this happens in Jesus' instructions to the man born blind in John 9.

John the Baptist sees Jesus and finally recognizes his true identity because he pays attention to God's specific revelation. John presents Jesus as the lamb of God who takes away the sin of the world, and his disciples begin following him. How will the blind man come to see and believe?

Jesus knows the truest identities of his disciples, causing them to feel a special connection and desire to follow him. He invites them to "come and see" (Jn 1:39, 46), assuring Nathaniel that he "will see the heavens opened and angels of God ascending and descending upon the Son of Man" (Jn 1:51). This 'seeing' prepares us for our story of the recovery of sight of the man blind from birth (Jn 9), the sixth of seven signs documented in John's Gospel.

John's Gospel highlights seven signs (*sēmeion*) that are not recognized or received by everyone, much like the word. Yet these signs and many others were recorded "so that you may believe that Jesus is the Christ, the Son of God; and that believing you may have life in his name"

(Jn 20:30-31). Belief in Jesus results from the each of the seven signs. You'll see how this happens in our story once the blind man comes to know Jesus.

Jesus' disciples believe in him when they witness his first sign, the turning of water into wine at a wedding feast. Only the servants who obey his instructions, and Jesus' newly-initiated disciples and mother witness the miracle—and the bridegroom gets the credit for saving the best wine till the end (Jn 2:1-11).

Jesus' second sign consists of confronting the injustice of the temple system in Jerusalem by driving merchants and bankers out, overturning their tables (Jn 2:12-17). In Jerusalem, "many believed in his name, observing his signs which he was doing" (Jn 2:23).

Nicodemus, a Pharisee, comes to Jesus by night, convinced by the signs that God is with him (Jn 3:2). Jesus tells him he must be born again if he wants to see the Kingdom of God, and that he can only enter the Kingdom by being born of water and the Spirit (Jn 3:3,5). Jesus clarifies that judgment is revealed in "that the light has come into the world, and men loved the darkness rather than the light, for their deeds were evil. For everyone who does evil hates the light, and does not come to the light for fear that his deeds will be exposed. But he who practices the truth comes to the Light, so that his deeds may be manifested as having been wrought in God" (Jn 3:19-21).

Jesus goes to Galilee, passing through Samaria where he encounters a Samaritan woman at a well. He offers her "living water," prophesying over her in a way that causes her to feel 'known" and reveals himself to her as the Christ. She tells her community about him, and is welcomed to share his liberating message with her fellow Samaritan villagers (Jn 4:1-45).

Jesus' third sign happens when he heals the son of another outsider, a royal official in Cana (Jn 4:46-54), by speaking a word from a distance, before heading back to Jerusalem to attend a feast.

Jesus' fourth sign is the healing of a man lame for 38 years by giving him instructions to "rise, take up your bed and walk" (Jn 5:1-15). This man once lame is then persecuted by religious authorities for carrying his bed on the Sabbath. He doesn't even know that it was Jesus who healed him until Jesus finds him later, instructing him to "not sin anymore, so that nothing worse happens to you" (Jn 5:13-14). The authorities respond by seeking to kill Jesus for breaking the Sabbath and identifying himself with God (Jn 5:18). Jesus insists that he can do nothing of himself, unless it is something he "sees" the Father doing (Jn 5:19).

Jesus' fifth sign occurs when he feeds 5000 people with only five barley loaves and two fish (Jn 6:1-5). There he invites people into deeper communion with himself as the Passover lamb, and many are offended (Jn 5:35-71).

Before Jesus' seventh sign, the raising of Lazarus from the dead (Jn 11), which causes the religious leaders to seek to kill him, we have John 9's presentation of Jesus' sixth sign—the healing and recruitment of a man born blind. Let's see what this story has to say to us today.

Reading John 9

In this story we see Jesus breaking the rules to heal and empower a person who meets no particular requirements. Jesus himself is on the run. But he still models and mobilizes the man healed from blindness, his disciples and us to like action.

This fresh reading was triggered by including the final verse of John 8 in the story of Jesus' healing of the man born blind.

"Therefore they picked up stones to throw at him, but Jesus hid himself and went out of the temple" (8:59).

Jesus was on the run from religious leaders who sought to administer the death penalty there in the temple.

"What were they doing and how did Jesus respond?" I ask the participants of our Wednesday afternoon Bible study.

"They picked up stones to throw at him. Jesus hid and got away fast," someone responds.

I then invite someone to read John 9:1.

"As he passed by, he saw a man blind from birth."

"So what happens right then when Jesus was on the run?," I ask.

Someone points out the obvious, but it suddenly looks different. Jesus is on the run, but as he passes a man blind from birth he *sees* him.

I ask our group how many of them remember actually running from the police or an enemy. A number of them nod their heads or raise their hands.

"Would it be normal to take note of a blind or unhoused person on the side of the road if you were on the run?" I ask.

"No way! My adrenaline would be pumping and all I'd be doing is trying to get away," someone says.

"I'd be looking in the rear-view mirror," says another.

"So even though Jesus is running for his life, hiding from the authorities, he's chill enough to still notice people in need around him," I say. "Let's see what happens next in verse 2." Someone reads:

"And his disciples asked him, "Rabbi, who sinned, this man or his parents, that he would be born blind?"

"How do the disciples view God based on their question?" I ask the group.

Someone mentions that the disciples think God must be looking for someone to blame in order to punish the guilty. Someone else asks how a newborn baby could sin, and says the disciples seem to view God as unfair.

"Would God actually punish an innocent infant with blindness due to his/her own sin or the parent's sin?" someone asks.

"Do people today see God as blaming and punishing, harsh and unfair?" I ask.

People say that many see God as unjust, and as only blessing those who fulfill the requirements in order to deserve benefits. They themselves often see God that way! What about you?

Let's see how Jesus responds," I say, inviting someone to read John 9:3.

"Jesus answered, "It was neither that this man sinned, nor his parents; but it was so that the works of God might be displayed in him."

"So how does Jesus respond exactly here?" I ask. "Jesus doesn't blame anyone—the man or his parents," someone says.

"Jesus sees the man's blindness as an opportunity for God to act.

At this point I invite people to look back in John 8 to see why the Jewish religious leaders were trying to stone Jesus in the first place.

Jesus had challenged the religious leaders' view of God, clearly stating that God was his Father.

"If God were your Father, you would love me, for I proceeded forth and have come from God, for I have not even come on my own initiative, but he sent me" (John 8:42).

Jesus here fulfills what was stated earlier in John 1:18. "No one has ever seen God. It is the only Son, himself God, who is close to the Father's heart, who has made him known" (NRSV).

Next, I summarize, emphasizing to our group that Jesus is on the run from the religious leaders, who are trying to execute him for identifying himself with God. And as God, Jesus is now refusing to cast blame on the blind man. Instead, he's explaining that the man's blindness from birth as an opportunity to engage in a liberating work. On top of that, Jesus deliberately includes his disciples then and now in God's saving action. I invite someone to read the next verses, which broadens Jesus' action to include the disciples—and you and me.

"We must work the works of him who sent me as long as it is day; night is coming when no one can work. While I am in the world, I am the Light of the world" (John 9:4-5).

Jesus includes his disciples in the "we" when he says: "we must work the works of him who sent me," I continue.

Jesus refuses to leave a blind man beside the road, judged as condemned by God because of someone's sin. Instead, he steps forward as the Light of the world, bringing his followers along with them, including us in his mission. Let's see what he does next," I suggest, inviting someone to read John 9:6-7.

"When he had said this, he spat on the ground, and made clay of the spittle, and applied the clay to his eyes, and said to him, "Go, wash in the pool of Siloam" (which is translated, Sent). So he went away and washed, and came back seeing."

We notice together that Jesus doesn't introduce himself to the blind man. He doesn't state his name, mention that he's the Son of God, God incarnate, or Lamb of God who takes away the sin of the world. Jesus crassly spits on the ground, makes mud with the spit, applies it to the man's eyes and tells him to wash in a pool called Siloam (Sent).

"What happened after this?" I ask our group.

"The blind man found his way to pool, washed the mud off his eyes and could see," someone says.

"He did what Jesus said, going to the pool called "Sent," and washing the mud off his eyes," another says.

"Yes," I affirm, and we'll see later that this man was right there being recruited by Jesus as a kind of spokesman, or prophet, because he ends up challenging the religious leaders themselves.

I then rapidly summarize how the Pharisees summon the man and question him and then his parents. Then they criticize Jesus for breaking the rules by healing on the Sabbath, and engage in a hostile back and forth conversation with the increasingly vocal man before they throw him out of their group, telling him: "You were born entirely in sins, and are you teaching us?" (8:34).

The answer here seems to be no and yes. No, Jesus has cleared the man of being born entirely in sins. And yes, the man is teaching the Pharisees themselves, since Jesus had sent him and he had responded, receiving his sight. Now he had stepped into his vocation, teaching the Pharisees themselves!

Yet we also notice that the Pharisees here exclude this man, cancelling him completely by answering the disciples' original question to Jesus about why the man was born blind. They blame him and his parents in their judgement: "you were born entirely in sins," and then they ex-communicate him.

"So what is God like if Jesus reveals God? What were the requirements for the blind man to recover his sight and join Jesus' missionary movement?" I ask.

"Did he have to believe that Jesus was the Son of God, confess and repent of his sins, be born again or follow him?" "Did he have to go to go to detox, get clean and sober, get into a treatment program, attend church, or pay his court fines or child support as pre-requisites? I prod.

Everyone is shaking their heads enthusiastically "no," and stating the beautiful obvious, which is very good news for people accustomed to having to comply with the many requirements of our criminal justice and social service systems, housing applications and job demands. Jesus reveals a God who sees us and loves us right where we're at. No questions asked. This love effects change—healing for this man born blind! Jesus shows that God is recruiting us all to engage with him in his Father's liberating works.

I invite people to read Jesus' final encounter with the man in John 4:35-40.

"Jesus heard that they had put him out, and finding him, he said, "Do you believe in the Son of Man?" He answered, "Who is he, Lord, that I may believe in him?" Jesus said to him, "You have both seen him, and he is the one who is talking with you." And he said, "Lord, I believe." And he worshiped him. And Jesus said, "For judgment I came into this world, so that those who do not see may see, and that those who see may become blind." Those of the Pharisees who were with him heard these things and said to him, "We are not blind too, are we?" Jesus said to them, "If you were blind, you would have no sin; but since you say, 'We see,' your sin remains."

We talk together about how Jesus himself found the man after he'd sent him, and he recovered his sight, asking him if he believed in the Son of Man, that is himself. Since the man still didn't know Jesus, he asks Jesus "Who is he, Lord, that I may believe in him?" When Jesus tells the man that he's seen him and that he's the guy talking to him right then and there, the man believes and worships him. We then see that there may be a kind of requirement to benefit from Jesus— recognizing and admitting that we ourselves are blind, in need of Jesus to open our eyes! This was something the religious leaders were not willing to do, so they were stuck with their sin.

RESPOND TO THE JOURNEY: WATCH, PRAY, MINISTER

We'd started our Bible study with the door open to keep the air circulating due to a recent Covid upsurge. Midway through our discussion my wife Gracie had closed the door so as to shut out afternoon road noise that was making it hard to hear.

Minutes before this last discussion about Jesus' unconditional healing, Gracie had gotten up and opened the door again. Almost immediately, two men stepped in, one of whom we knew and had been quite worried about because he's smoking fentanyl. The other man we didn't know stood at the door and asked us all a question that shocked us due to its timeliness.

"Hey, can you tell me what the requirements are to be part of this church?" he said.

"There are no requirements," several people said all at once.

"Hey, come on in and join us now if you'd like," I said, while others ushered them inside and offered each of them a chair in our circle.

The man we knew peeked in but then stepped back out onto the sidewalk, and his friend then said:

"Hey, I'm really worried about my cousin, and about myself too. I know that we need God. I sure do! Maybe now's not going to work, but I'll be back," before running after his cousin who was heading down the street.

We all prayed for these two men then and there, before wrapping up the Bible study by reading later in the story how Jesus came back and found the once-blind man he'd healed.

Before wrapping up our time with prayer, we read together how Jesus found the man, asking him: "Do you believe in the Son of Man?"

We laugh about how the man has no idea who the Son of Man, is but humbly says: "Who is he Lord that I may believe in him?"

I'm deeply moved by how Jesus doesn't give a big explanation from Scripture but simply tells him: "You have both seen him, and he is the one who is talking with you" (8:37).

The man's response: "Lord, I believe," and his worship of Jesus is something we're all ready to do then and there.

I ask whether there's anyone in need of prayer before we wrap up. A man who'd suffered as a Vietnam veteran two-years clean off crack cocaine says he needs prayer for COPD, a chronic lung condition that makes it hard for him to speak beyond a faint whisper. We gather around and lay hands on him, praying for his healing. Almost immediately he notices a big change. He is astonished as he starts to breathe more freely, and we notice the volume of his voice increases significantly. We all marvel at the beautiful presence of Jesus moving in our midst, delighted by the radical goodness of God.

1.

JESUS' GREAT COMMISSION

MATTHEW 28:18-20

Study Guide	Notes

Background

In Matthew's gospel Jesus teaches and embodies his message of holistic liberation, announcing and enacting the Kingdom of God. After his baptism and temptation, Jesus goes to Galilee where he calls fishermen and a tax-collector as disciples. He teaches them and the crowds, sending his disciples out to preach, heal and cast out evil spirits. After Jesus' death and resurrection, he meets up with his disciples for a final conversation on a mountain in Galilee. There he commissions them with precise instructions to expand his mission to the nations. These instructions now apply to each and every follower of Jesus.

Introduction

When two of Jesus' women followers, Mary Magdalene and the other Mary come to the tomb after Jesus' death and burial, they are met by an angel. The angel gives them instructions about where the resurrected Jesus wants to meet up with his eleven remaining disciples—on a mountain in Galilee. It is there that he shares with them his final words about their mission, which is often called "The Great Commission."

Read Matthew 28:5-7

"The angel said to the women, "Do not be afraid; for I know that you are looking for Jesus who has been crucified. "He is not here, for he has risen, just as he said. Come, see the place where he was lying. "Go quickly and tell his disciples that he has risen from the dead; and behold, he is going ahead of you into Galilee. There you will see him; behold, I have told you."

Study Guide	Notes

Question 1

What does the angel tell the women who come to the empty tomb?

He tells them not to be afraid, that Jesus is risen.

He invites them to come see for themselves where he was laying.

He tells them to go quickly and tell his disciples that he's risen from the dead.

Jesus is going ahead of them to Galilee and they will see him.

In the next verse Jesus himself meets them and tells them the same things.

Question 2

Why do you think the angel tells the women to "go quickly"?

Explanation

Soon after this in Matthew 28:11-15 the soldiers who had sealed the tomb report what happened. The authorities then gave them money to tell people his disciples had stollen Jesus' body. The angel tells the women to go quickly so the disciples know Jesus has risen from the dead and they can leave Jerusalem for Galilee, before the false report that they'd stolen the body gets out.

Read Matthew 28:8-10

"And they left the tomb quickly with fear and great joy and ran to report it to his disciples. And behold, Jesus met them and greeted them. And they came up and took hold of his feet and worshiped him. Then Jesus said to them, "Do not be afraid; go and take word to my brethren to leave for Galilee, and there they will see me.""

Study Guide	Notes
Question 3 ? What happens next? How did the women respond and what did Jesus say?	The two women leave the tomb quickly, running, with "fear and great joy," to report the news to his disciples. Jesus himself met them and greeted them. They took hold of his feet and worshipped him. Jesus tells them to not be afraid, but to take word to "my brothers." Jesus repeats instructions of the angel, with some important changes. He tells them: "leave for Galilee," where "you will see me."
Explanation ✓	The angel calls Jesus' followers "his disciples," Jesus calls them "my brothers." "Tell his disciples" vs. "take word to my brothers." Here the Greek *apaggellō*, means "to report, announce, inform." (Mk 5:14, 19; Mk 16:10; Lk 7:22; 18:37; Acts 11:13). Women pass on critical information about "where" disciples are going to see Jesus— back at the original site (Galilee) where the movement began.
Question 4 ? If you were Jesus' original disciples and had just witnessed his arrest and execution, what would you be thinking and feeling upon hearing this news?	You might find this unbelievable. You might think the women are crazy. You would likely feel completely overwhelmed, confused and excited.

Study Guide	Notes

Explanation-Galilee ✓

In Matthew 4:12-15 Matthew describes Jesus' move to Galilee.

"Now when Jesus heard that John had been taken into custody, he withdrew into Galilee; and leaving Nazareth, he came and settled in Capernaum, which is by the sea, in the region of Zebulun and Naphtali. This was to fulfill what was spoken through Isaiah the prophet: "The land of Zebulun and the land of Naphtali, by the way of the sea, beyond the Jordan, Galilee of the Gentiles— "The people who were sitting in darkness saw a great light, and those who were sitting in the land and shadow of death, upon them a light dawned" (Mt 4:12-15).

Read Matthew 28:16-17 📖

"But the eleven disciples proceeded to Galilee, to the mountain which Jesus had designated. When they saw him, they worshiped him; but some were doubtful."

Question 5 ?

Where did the disciples go and what happened?

To Galilee, to meet Jesus on a mountain he designated.

When they saw Jesus, they worshipped him.

Some of them doubted.

Question 6 ?

How would you feel about meeting up with someone you had followed, who had been executed but was now alive?

You would likely feel a mixture of fear, doubt and excitement.

Study Guide	**Notes**
Read Matthew 28:18 📖	
"And Jesus came up and spoke to them, saying, "All authority has been given to me in heaven and on earth."	
Question 7 ?	
What did Jesus do and say here? What do you think it means that Jesus has been given all authority?	All authority has been given to him in heaven and earth.
	Apparently the Father gave Jesus this authority, but that is not mentioned.
Read Matthew 28:19 📖	
"Go therefore and make disciples of all the nations, baptizing them in the name of the Father and the Son and the Holy Spirit."	
Question 8 ?	
What did tell his disciples to do here?	Go and make disciples of all the nations.
	Baptize these disciples in the name of the Father, the Son and the Holy Spirit.

Study Guide	Notes
Explanation ✓	Literally Jesus says here: "As you go, make disciples…" This suggests that Jesus considers making disciples a core activity of disciples as we go about our normal daily living.
	The Greek verb translated "go" is *poreuomai*, which means "to move from one place to another," and "to travel, to journey, to be on one's way."[1] The grammatical form here is the plural aorist passive participle, best translated: "as you move from one place to another" or "as you travel."
	Make disciples comes from the imperative of the Greek verb *mathēteuō*, which means "to cause someone to become a disciple or follower of — 'to make disciples, to cause people to become followers.'"[2]
Question 9 ?	
How did Jesus himself make disciples as he went?	He called them, taught them and demonstrated the Kingdom of God through healing people, casting out evil spirits and other signs.
Explanation ✓	We can carefully read through the gospel of Matthew, taking note of how Jesus went about calling and training his disciples. In Matthew 4:18-22 and 9:9-13 Jesus calls fishermen and a tax collector.

1. J. P. Louw, and Eugene Albert Nida, eds. *Greek-English Lexicon of the New Testament*, Accordance electronic ed.,15.10; 15.18.

2. Louw and Nida, *Greek-English Lexicon*, 36.37.

Study Guide	Notes

Read Matthew 4:18-19 📖

"Now as Jesus was walking by the Sea of Galilee, he saw two brothers, Simon who was called Peter, and Andrew his brother, casting a net into the sea; for they were fishermen. And he said to them, "Follow me, and I will make you fishers of men.""

Question 10 ?

What does this story show us about how Jesus called disciples?

Jesus went and found people right where they were working. In this case he sees fishermen casting nets into the sea. They were looking for fish, for food and income.

Jesus calls them to follow him and commits to making them into fishers of people.

Read Matthew 9:9 📖

"As Jesus went on from there, he saw a man called Matthew, sitting in the tax collector's booth; and he said to him, "Follow me!" And he got up and followed him."

Question 11 ?

How does Jesus recruit a disciple here?

Jesus went to where Matthew, a tax-collector was collecting his taxes. He invites him to follow him and Matthew follows him.

Study Guide	Notes

Explanation

After calling Matthew the tax-collector Jesus went and ate at Matthew's house, and "many tax collectors and sinners came and were dining with Jesus and his disciples" (Mt 9:10). In response to the complaints of Jewish religious leaders called Pharisees that Jesus at with sinners, he said: "It is not those who are healthy who need a physician, but those who are sick. "But go and learn what this means: 'I desire compassion, and not sacrifice,' for I did not come to call the righteous, but sinners" (Mt 9:12-13). This shows that Jesus recruits disciples from among those rejected by society due to their behavior and lifestyle.

Question 12

Why is it important to baptize new disciples in the name of the Father and the Son and the Holy Spirit?

Stepping into our baptismal identity involves knowing God as Father, Son, and Holy Spirit.

When Jesus is baptized in Matthew 3:13-17 the heavens were opened to him, and he saw the Spirit of God descending like a dove and coming to rest on him, and the Father said: "This is my beloved Son, with whom I am well pleased.

Study Guide	Notes

Explanation

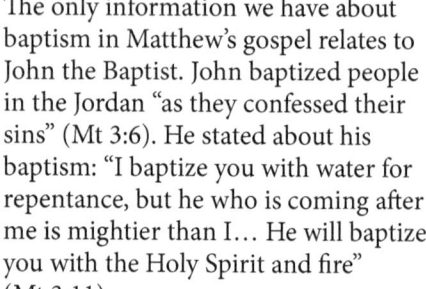

The only information we have about baptism in Matthew's gospel relates to John the Baptist. John baptized people in the Jordan "as they confessed their sins" (Mt 3:6). He stated about his baptism: "I baptize you with water for repentance, but he who is coming after me is mightier than I… He will baptize you with the Holy Spirit and fire" (Mt 3:11).

When Jesus was baptized, as he came up from the water "the heavens were opened, and he saw the spirit of God descending as a dove and lighting on him, and behold a voice out of the heavens said, "This is my beloved Son, in whom I am well pleased" (Mt 3:16-17).

Apart from Matthew, the book of Acts describes baptisms, as when Peter addresses the crowd on the day of Pentecost: "Repent, and each of you be baptized in the name of Jesus Christ for the forgiveness of your sins; and you will receive the gift of the Holy Spirit" (Acts 2:38).

Acts describes people being baptized in the name of Jesus, and then subsequently having hands laid on them to receive the Holy Spirit (Acts 8:16-17).

Jesus teaches about relationship with the Father throughout Matthew's Gospel (Mt 5:16, 45, 48; 6:1, 4, 6, 8, 9, 14, 15, 18, 26, 32; 7:11, 21…), as well as the Spirit (Mt 1:21; 3:11, 16; 4:1; 12:18, 28, 31, 32).

Study Guide	Notes

Read Matthew 28:20

"Teaching them to observe all that I commanded you; and lo, I am with you always, even to the end of the age."

Question 13

What are disciples to teach those they baptize?

To observe all that Jesus had commanded them.

Explanation

Disciples are to teach others to "observe" or "keep" Jesus' commandments. The Greek verb, *tēreō* means "to cause to continue, retain, keep," or "to obey, to keep commandments."[3]

Jesus never commands his disciples, using the verb *entello*, which is used here. In John's Gospel Jesus states: "You are my friends if you do what I command you" (Jn 15:14). "This I command you, that you love one another" (Jn 15:17).

In Matthew's Gospel Jesus' many direct words to his disciples in his teaching and ministry can be considered his commands. These can be found through reading through the gospel-which serves as a kind of disciple-training manual.

---

3. Louw and Nida, *Greek-English Lexicon*,13.32; 36:19.

Study Guide	Notes

Question 14   ?

What had Jesus commanded according to Matthew's Gospel?

Here is a sampling of Jesus' direct commands

"Repent, for the Kingdom of Heaven is at hand" (Mt 4:17).

"Follow me, and I will make you fishers of people" (Mt 4:19).

"Let your light shine before people…" (Mt 5:16).

"Love your enemies and pray for those who persecute you" (Mt 5:44).

"Beware of practicing your righteousness before people to be noticed by them" (Mt 6:1).

"When you pray, go into your inner room, close your door and pray to your Father who is in secret" (Mt 6:6).

"Pray, then, in this way: 'Our Father who is in heaven…'" (Mt 6:9).

"Do not store up for yourselves treasures on earth… Store up for yourselves treasures in heaven" (Mt 6:19, 20).

"Do not be worried about your life… But seek first his kingdom and his righteousness…" (Mt 6:25, 33).

"Do not judge, so that you will not be judged" (Mt 7:1).

"Ask and it will be given to you; seek, and you will find; knock, and it will be opened to you" (Mt 7:7).

"Go and learn what this means: 'I desire compassion, and not sacrifice'" (Mt 9:13).

Study Guide	Notes
	"Come to me, all who are weary and heavy-laden, and I will give you rest. Take my yoke upon you and learn from me" (Mt 11:28-29).
	"Watch out and beware of the leaven of the Pharisees and Sadducees" (Mt 16:6).
	"See that you do not despise one of these little ones" (Mt 18:10).
	"You shall love the Lord your God with all your heart, and with all your soul, and with all your mind… You shall love your neighbor as yourself" (Mt 22:37-38).
	"Therefore, be on the alert, for you do not know which day your Lord is coming" (Mt 24:42).
	"Take, eat; this is my body… Drink from it all of you, for this is my blood of the covenant, which is poured our for many for the forgiveness of sins" (Mt 26:26-28).
	"Keep watching and praying that you may not enter into temptation; the spirit is willing, but the flesh is weak" (Mt 26:41).
	"Put your sword back into its place; for all those who take up the sword shall perish by the sword" (Mt 26:52).

Question 15

How would you go about learning, practicing, and teaching Jesus' commandments today?

Study Guide	Notes
Read Matthew 28:20b 📖	
"And lo, I am with you always, even to the end of the age."	
Question 16 ?	
What are Jesus' final words here? Why do you think these are his last words? How do these words encourage you?	"I am with you always, even to the end of the age."
	Jesus assures his disciples that he is alive and will be with them (and us) all the time and forever.
	Following Jesus is not just about following teaching. Jesus' presence through the Holy Spirit is with disciples to guide them and us all the time.
Invitation ⟶	Invite people to pray together to Jesus, thanking him for his teaching, committing to seeking to learn and practice his commands. Invite people to receive the Holy Spirit to guide and encourage them on their journey.

2.

THE MISSION OF ISAIAH'S SERVANT OF THE LORD

ISAIAH 42:1-8

Study Guide	Notes
Background	The Book of Isaiah is a collection of prophecies that span hundreds of years. Isaiah 1-39 consists of prophetic critique and calls to conversion addressed to Israel's Southern tribes (Judah and Benjamin), before Jerusalem was destroyed and the people were carried off into exile in Babylon.
	Isaiah 40-55 addresses God's people in their exile in Babylon. There God recruits them for universal mission. The Servant of the Lord provides a role description for missionaries to contemporary exiles. Isaiah 42:1-7 is the first of four "servant poems" describing the servant's identity and mission. This mission is further clarified in the Isaiah 49:1-7; 50:4-11 and 52:13-53:12.
Introduction	In Isaiah 42:1-8 God clarifies the Servant's identity and mission before the nations. In Isaiah 40-55 the Servant of the Lord is Israel in her exiled, enslaved state in Babylon. Yet Isaiah's prophecies present God's people as not in any way disqualified by their failures, blindness or sin. Rather God's call proves irrevocable and recruitment continuous.
Read Isaiah 42:1 📖	
"Behold, my Servant, whom I uphold; my chosen one in whom my soul delights. I have put my Spirit upon him; he will bring forth justice to the nations."	

Study Guide	Notes
Question 1	The Servant is the Lord's Servant— "my Servant"
What do we know about the Servant from this verse?	Chosen
	The Lord's soul delights in the Servant
	The Lord has put his Spirit upon him
	The Servant will bring forth justice to the nations.
Explanation	Earlier in Isaiah 41:10 the Lord uses the same language for Israel in a text where God is described as taking the Servant from the ends of the earth: "Surely I will uphold you with my righteous right hand."
Read Isaiah 41:8-9	
"But you, Israel, my Servant, Jacob whom I have chosen, descendant of Abraham my friend, you whom I have taken from the ends of the earth, and called from its remotest parts, and said to you, 'You are my Servant, I have chosen you and not rejected you"	
Question 2	The Servant is identified here as Israel and Jacob.
Who is the Servant in these verses? What does God say about the Servant? What does that tell us about God?	God has chosen the Servant, who is a descendant of Abraham.
	God calls the Servant "my friend," and says "I have taken you from the ends of the earth and from its remotest parts.
	God repeats these words: "You are my Servant... chosen... not rejected."

Study Guide	Notes

Read Isaiah 44:21 and 45:4 📖

"Remember these things, O Jacob, and Israel, for you are my Servant; I have formed you, you are my Servant, O Israel, you will not be forgotten by me" (Is 44:21).

"For the sake of Jacob my Servant, and Israel My chosen one, I have also called you by your name; I have given you a title of honor though you have not known me" (Is 45:4).

Question 3 ?

What are the different names the Servant is called in these verses and what does that tell us about God sees him?

Refers to Israel and Jacob—terms for the Jewish people

Chosen (by God)… not rejected

"My friend"

Taken [by God] from the ends of the earth, called

"I [God] have formed you"

Not forgotten

"I [God] have called you by name"

"I have given you a title of honor"

Study Guide	Notes

Explanation

The Servant's identity in Isaiah

- The Hebrew term *eved*, occurs 40x in Isaiah
- Isaiah 1-39 *eved* never refers overtly to Israel
- *Eved* in Isaiah 40-55 refers to Israel is the majority of cases (41:8,9; 42:19, 19; 43:10; 44:1, 2, 21, 21, 26; 45:4; 48:20; 42:19, 19; 49:3).
- Select number of cases where *eved* is more enigmatic—and cannot be Israel (42:1, 49:5, 6, 7; 50:10; 52:13; 53:11).
- Every occurrence of *eved* after Isaiah 53 is plural

Read Isaiah 42:18-22

"Hear, you deaf! And look, you blind, that you may see. Who is blind but my Servant, or so deaf as my messenger whom I send? Who is so blind as he that is at peace with me, or so blind as the Servant of the Lord? You have seen many things, but you do not observe them; your ears are open, but none hears. The Lord was pleased for His righteousness' sake to make the law great and glorious. But this is a people plundered and despoiled; all of them are trapped in caves, or are hidden away in prisons; they have become a prey with none to deliver them, and a spoil, with none to say, "Give them back!""

Study Guide	Notes
Question 4 ?	The Servant is described as being blind and deaf.
What do these verses tell us about the Servant?	God's people are "plundered and despoiled," "trapped in caves or hidden away in prisons"- with no one to rescue them.
Question 5 ?	
Who are today's equivalents?	Prisoners, addicts, people struggling with mental illness…
Question 6 ?	
What does God's choice of the Servant tell us about God?	God is merciful and gracious, choosing those the world considers unqualified.
Read Isaiah 42:2-3 📖	
"He will not cry out or raise his voice, Nor make his voice heard in the street."	
"A bruised reed he will not break And a dimly burning wick he will not extinguish; he will faithfully bring forth justice."	

Study Guide	Notes
Question 7 ?	The Servant will not:
What actions does the Servant not do?	
What means does the Servant use? What would that look like now?	– Cry out or raise his voice
	– The Servant's voice will not be heard in the street—publicly, out in the open.
	– The Servant will not break a bruised read or extinguish a faintly-burning wick.
	The Servant will faithfully bring forth justice.
Explanation ✓	A bruised reed refers directly to Egypt in 2 Kings 18:21 "Now behold, you rely on the staff of this crushed reed, even on Egypt." See also Isaiah 36:6. The Lord's Servant will not further break something that is already down or under judgment.
	A dimly burning wick likely refers to the Lord's defeat of the Egyptians in the sea, "They have been quenched *and* extinguished like a wick" (Is 43:17). In contrast, the Servant will not defeat adversaries in this way.
Read Isaiah 42:4 📖	
"He will not be disheartened or crushed until he has established justice in the earth; and the coastlands will wait expectantly for his law."	
Question 8 ?	
What is the Servant's mission here?	To establish justice in the earth.
	To bring God's law to the coastlands.

Study Guide	Notes

Explanation

The underlaying term translated "law" here is *torah*, with means "direction, instruction, law,"[1] or teaching, and can refer to the first five books of the Hebrew Bible (Pentateuch). In Isaiah *Torah* always refers to the Lord's Torah (Is 1:10; 2:3; 5:24; 8:16, 20; 24:5; 30:9; 42:21, 24;51:4, 7), identifying the Servant with the Lord himself.

Read Isaiah 42:5-6

"Thus says God the Lord, who created the heavens and stretched them out, who spread out the earth and its offspring, who gives breath to the people on it and spirit to those who walk in it, "I am the Lord, I have called you in righteousness, I will also hold you by the hand and watch over you, and I will appoint you as a covenant to the people, as a light to the nations,"

Question 9   ?

What more do these verses tell us about God and about the Servant's mission?

The God who calls the Servant is the Creator of the heavens and giver of life and spirit to all humans.

The Lord speaks personally to the Servant, saying 'I have called you in righteousness."

The Lord tells the Servant "I will hold you by the hand and watch over you."

The Lord will appoint the Servant as a covenant to the people and a light to the nations.

---

1. F. Brown, S. R. Driver, and C. A. Briggs, *A Hebrew and English Lexicon of the Old Testament*, abridged, Oxford: Clarendon Press, 1907, 8451, 8452.

Study Guide	Notes
Read Isaiah 42:7 📖	
"To open blind eyes, to bring out prisoners from the dungeon and those who dwell in darkness from the prison."	
Question 10 ?	
What more do these verses tell us about the Servant's mission?	The Lord personally appoints the Servant to open blind eyes, bring out prisoners from captivity, and those living in darkness from prison.
Read Isaiah 42:8 📖	
"I am the Lord, that is my name; I will not give my glory to another, nor my praise to graven images."	
Question 11 ?	
To whom does God give glory?	The Lord gives glory to none other than the people God is raising up from having been down, imprisoned, or oppressed. God empowers those considered blind and deaf to become agents of liberation.
Invitation ⟶	Invite people to consider whether they have felt blind, deaf, imprisoned, or in any way stuck, but who now feel recruited to engage in the ministry of the Servant.
	Close with a time of prayer, affirming your desire to be part of the Servant's mission.

3.

JESUS PUBLICLY
STATES HIS MISSION

LUKE 4:14-21

Study Guide	Notes
Introduction	In Luke's Gospel Jesus inaugurates his ministry in his hometown synagogue in Nazareth by publicly reading Isaiah 61:1-2. Jesus declares this prophecy regarding the coming Servant of the Lord and his liberating mission as being fulfilled by himself. The details Jesus highlights from this powerful prophetic announcement set the course of Jesus' movement, which continues today.
Background	In Luke's Gospel Jesus is baptized by John the Baptist in the Jordan River. There the Holy Spirit descends "in bodily form like a dove," and the Father says: "You are my beloved Son, in you I am well-pleased" (Lk 3:22). Full of the Holy Spirit, Jesus is led by the Spirit in the wilderness, where he is tempted by the devil while he fasts forty days and nights. The devil sought to direct Jesus to work miracles (turning stones into bread), challenging him to prove his identity as the Son of God. He offered to give Jesus all the kingdoms of the world in exchange for his total allegiance (Lk 3:6-7), and challenged him to depend on angels to protect him to accomplish spectacular feats. Jesus overcame the temptations, and began his mission "in the power of the Spirit."

Read Luke 4:14-15 📖

"And Jesus returned to Galilee in the power of the Spirit, and news about him spread through all the surrounding district. And he began teaching in their synagogues and was praised by all."

Study Guide	Notes

Question 1 ?

Where did Jesus go and what's said about him and what he did?

Jesus returned to Galilee.

He was "in the power of the Spirit"

News spread about him everywhere.

He taught in the Jewish synagogues

He was praised by all.

Explanation ✓

Galilee was in the remote Northeast part of Israel, far from the main city and religious center, Jerusalem.

Read Luke 4:16-17 📖

"And he came to Nazareth, where he had been brought up; and as was his custom, he entered the synagogue on the Sabbath, and stood up to read. And the book of the prophet Isaiah was handed to him. And he opened the book and found the place where it was written,"

Question 2 ?

Where did Jesus go and what did he do?

Jesus came to Nazareth, his hometown.

He entered the synagogue on the Sabbath.

He stood up to read, and he was given the book of Isaiah

Jesus chose and deliberately found a specific passage that he read.

Study Guide	Notes

Read Luke 4:18a 📖

"The Spirit of the Lord is upon me, because he anointed me to preach the Gospel to the poor."

Question 3 ?

The Spirit of the Lord is upon Jesus and he is anointed for what purpose?

To preach the good news to the poor.

Explanation ✓

"Preach the Gospel" comes from one Greek verb, *euaggelizo*, meaning "to communicate good news concerning something."[1]

The poor (*ptōchos*) refers to the needy, those "destitute of wealth, influence, position, honors; lowly, afflicted."[2]

Question 4 ?

Who are the poor in your community? What would "good news" look like to them?

Read Luke 4:18b 📖

"He has sent me to proclaim release to the captives, and recovery of sight to the blind, to set free those who are oppressed, to proclaim the favorable year of the Lord."

---

1. Louw and Nida, *Greek-English Lexicon*, 33.215

2. Joseph Henry Thayer, *Thayer's Greek-English Lexicon of the New Testament*, Accordance electronic ed. New York: Harper and Brothers, 1889, 4434.2.

Study Guide	Notes

Question 5

What is the second action Isaiah describes here and who benefits?

Proclaiming release to the captives.

Explanation

In addition to the Spirit anointing Jesus to proclaim good news to the poor, a second, deliberate action involves being sent (*apostellō*)[3] to engage in the next four actions listed.

"Release" (*aphesis*) here means "release from captivity, pardon, cancelation of obligation or a punishment from guilt.[4] *Aphesis* often means forgiveness from sin in Luke's Gospel (Lk 1:77; 3:3; 24:47)

"Proclaiming" (*kerusso*) means to "announce, make known by a herald."[5]

Captives (*aichmalotos*) is used only here in the New Testament. In the Greek Old Testament it refers to prisoners of war or prisoners (Nm 21:9; Est 2:6; Am 7:11,17; Nah 3:10; Is 5:13; 46:2; Ez 30:18).

Question 6

Who are the captives today? What would it look like to proclaim release to them?

---

3. *Apostellō* means to "set apart, i.e. (by implication) to send out (properly, on a mission) literally or figuratively: — put in, send (away, forth, out), set (at liberty)." *Key Dictionary of the Greek New Testament*, OakTree Software, 2010, 649.

4. Walter Bauer, *A Greek-English Lexicon of the New Testament and Other Early Christian Literature*, Translated by William F. Arndt and F. Wilbur Gingrich, Chicago: University of Chicago Press, 1979, p. 125.

5. Bauer, *A Greek-English Lexicon*, p. 431.

Study Guide	Notes

Question 7 ?

What is the third action Jesus lists as he reads from Isaiah?

Proclaiming recovery of sight for the blind.

Explanation ✓

Recovery of sight (*anablepsis*) to the blind is associated with the coming Messiah. This phrase does not occur in the Hebrew version of Isaiah 61:1. The Greek Version (Septuagint) harmonizes with many places in Isaiah that describe the Lord's Servant as bringing sight to the blind.

Read Isaiah 29:18; 35:5; 42:7; 42:16[6] 📖

"On that day the deaf shall hear the words of a scroll, and as for those who are in the darkness and those who are in the fog, the eyes of the blind shall see" (Is 29:18).

"Then the eyes of the blind shall be opened, and the ears of the deaf shall hear" (Is 35:5).

"To open the eyes of the blind, to bring out from bonds those who are bound and from the prison house those who sit in darkness" (Is 42:7).

"And I will lead the blind by a road they have not known, and I will make them tread paths they had no knowledge of. I will turn the darkness into light for them and the crooked places into a straight path. I will do these things, and I will not forsake them" (Is 42:16).

"Hear, you that are deaf, and you that are blind, look up to see!" (Is 42:18).

6. These citations are from *The New English Translation of the Septuagint* (NETS), edited by Albert Pietersma and Benjamin C. Wright, NETS Text Edition: 2014. Copyright @2007 by International Organization for Septuagint and Cognate Studies, Inc. Used by permission of Oxford University Press, Version 3.9.

Study Guide	Notes

Question 8   ?

Who are the blind today? What would it like to proclaim recovery of sight?

Question 9   ?

What is the fourth action Jesus lists from Isaiah?

Setting free those who are oppressed.

Explanation ✓

Set free means literally "to send away (*apostellō*) free (*aphesis*) the oppressed," which is from the Septuagint of Isaiah 58:6.

"The oppressed" (*thrauō*) means "break in pieces"[7] referring to those "downtrodden, troubled, overwhelmed."[8]

Read Luke 4:19 📖

"To proclaim the favorable year of the Lord."

Explanation ✓

In Luke, Jesus emphasizes "proclaiming" the favorable year of the Lord. The term "favorable" (*dektos*), has the meaning "pertaining to that which is pleasing in view of its being acceptable — 'pleasing, acceptable.'"[9]

This refers to what's called the "Year of Jubilee," detailed in Leviticus 25:10-13, when debts are forgiven, land is returned to original owners, and land is to lay fallow. The Septuagint version shows the same language used in Luke 4:18-19, especially the word "release" (*aphesis*).

7. Bauer, *A Greek-English Lexicon*, p. 363.

8. Louw and Nida, *Greek-English Lexicon*, 22.22.

9. Louw and Nida, *Greek-English Lexicon*, 25.85.

Study Guide	**Notes**

"And you shall hallow the year, the fiftieth year, and you shall proclaim release (*aphesis*) on the land to all its inhabitants. It shall be a year of release (*aphesis*); a signal this shall be for you, and each one shall depart to his possession, and each shall depart to his clan. This is a signal of release (*aphesis*): the fiftieth year. It shall be a year for you" (Lev 25:10-11a).

Question 10 ?

What would it look like for this "favorable year of the Lord" to become a reality now?

Question 11 ?

What do these actions of the Spirit of the Lord tell us about God and the Spirit?

The Spirit of the Lord anoints Jesus to preach Good News to the poor. This shows God's special concern that the poor have liberating messages spoken to them by fellow human beings specially anointed by God for this purpose.

Read Luke 4:20-21 📖

"And he closed the book, gave it back to the attendant and sat down; and the eyes of all in the synagogue were fixed on him. And he began to say to them, "Today this Scripture has been fulfilled in your hearing.""

Question 12 ?

What do Jesus' words that this this Scripture is fulfilled right then and there before them suggest to the people and us?

That Jesus himself is the one the Spirit has anointed and sent to engage in these actions.

Jesus and the Spirit of the Lord are united in the same mission.

Study Guide	Notes

Read Luke 4:22 📖

"And all were speaking well of him, and wondering at the gracious words which were falling from his lips; and they were saying, "Is this not Joseph's son?""

Question 13 ?

How did people react to Jesus?

They were impressed with Jesus. At the same time they were <u>wondering</u> about "the gracious words coming from his mouth."

They asked the question: "Is this not Joseph's son?" They knew him as Joseph's son.

Explanation ✓

The people of Jesus' hometown, Nazareth focus on Jesus identity as Joseph's son. They show no awareness of Jesus identity as Son of God, clarified at his baptism. Nor do they see him as Israel's Messiah, though he cited Isaiah 61, and himself as fulfilling this Scripture announcing the Messiah.

Read Luke 4:23-24 📖

"And he said to them, "No doubt you will quote this proverb to me, 'Physician, heal yourself! Whatever we heard was done at Capernaum, do here in your hometown as well. And he said, "Truly I say to you, no prophet is welcome in his hometown."

Question 13 ?

What is Jesus saying to them here and why?

Jesus seems to interpret their "wondering" as discounting him,

Study Guide	Notes

Explanation

Jesus appears to be discerning prophetically that his fellow villagers want him to do miraculous deeds for them, that he appears to have been known for based on what he'd done in Capernaum. Is Jesus discerning that they see themselves as worthy and entitled, self-oriented rather than oriented towards others who are even more clearly the poor, prisoners, blind and oppressed?

Jesus calls them out, appearing to know that he is not welcomed as a prophet, a spokesman for God. He may be addressing their pride, self-righteousness, and victim-mindset, which is confirmed by what he says next.

Read Luke 4:25-26

"But I say to you in truth, there were many widows in Israel in the days of Elijah, when the sky was shut up for three years and six months, when a great famine came over all the land; and yet Elijah was sent to none of them, but only to Zarephath, in the land of Sidon, to a woman who was a widow."

Explanation

Jesus confronts his townspeople with his own observation about two of Israel's greatest prophets, Elijah and Elisha. He notes that these prophets were unable to do great miracles to benefit God's chosen people, but rather only unclean, outsider Gentiles and even a national enemy (Naaman).

Study Guide	Notes
Question 14 ?	Jesus emphasizes that one of Israel's most celebrated prophets, Elijah was sent by God to bless a Gentile (non-Jewish, pagan) widow in a neighboring, enemy country, the land of Sidon, rather than to one of Israel's many needy widows.
What example is Jesus offering his townspeople and why?	
	Jesus wants his townspeople to see how they can miss out on God's blessing mediated through someone they see as familiar, like himself, who is from Nazareth, who they might dismiss.
	Jesus also wants them to include people in God's blessing who they would normally see as unqualified and excluded.
Read Luke 4:27 📖	
"And there were many lepers in Israel in the time of Elisha the prophet; and none of them was cleansed, but only Naaman the Syrian."	
Question 15 ?	Here Jesus highlights that Israel's most famous prophet, Elisha cleansed a Syrian military commander, a national enemy, rather than healing an Israelite leper.
What example is Jesus offering here and why?	
	Like in the first example, Jesus is showing that his people can miss out on God's blessing for themselves like the people of Elisha's time, and that God desires to bless everyone, even national enemies.

Study Guide	Notes

Read Luke 4:28-30 📖

"And all the people in the synagogue were filled with rage as they heard these things; and they got up and drove him out of the city, and led him to the brow of the hill on which their city had been built, in order to throw him down the cliff. But passing through their midst, he went his way."

Question 16 ?

How did people react to Jesus' message and examples?

They were enraged and tried to throw him off a cliff.

Explanation ✓

Jesus is trying shift his people from being "self" oriented to "other" oriented.

Question 17 ?

Who might be today's equivalents of poor, prisoners, blind and oppressed that we or others would be offended should they be the focus of God's attention?

Terrorists, sex-offenders, criminals, national enemies, political opponents, personal enemies…

Question 18 ?

How does Jesus' mission statement here affect and include us?

Invitation ⟶

Invite people to consider whether they want to step into active agreement with Jesus mission statement. Consider praying for the Spirit of the Lord to anoint and send people into mission according to Jesus' priorities in this Scripture.

4.

JESUS SENDS THE SEVENTY OUT ON MISSION

LUKE 10:1-19

Study Guide	Notes

Introduction

In Luke's Gospel Jesus calls together his twelve disciples, giving them "power and authority over all the demons and to heal diseases" (Lk 9:1), sending them out to proclaim the Kingdom of God and to heal. He sends them with precise instructions about what not to take, and how they are to receive hospitality. Then in Luke 10:1ff Jesus movements grows. He appoints 70 (or 72) others, sending them out in pairs.

Read Luke 10:1 📖

"Now after this the Lord appointed seventy others, and sent them in pairs ahead of him to every city and place where he himself was going to come."

Question 1 ?

What does Jesus do here?

Jesus appoints seventy others and sends them ahead of him to each of the cities and places where he was going.

Explanation ✓

Some versions of the Bible have Jesus appointing and sending out 70 missionaries, while others have 72. This is based on differences between the Hebrew version of Genesis 10's list of nations, which numbers 70. There are 72 nations listed in the LXX (the Greek translation of the Old Testament). Jesus is emphasizing here that his mission extends to every nation in the world.

Study Guide	Notes
	Jesus sending of "others" reminds readers of the twelve disciples he had sent out on a similar mission in Luke 9. The movement from twelve to 70 refers to both Israel's mission through twelve tribes and the empowerment of the seventy elders who Moses appointed and the Spirit empowered (Nu 11:24-25). Jesus sends the seventy to prepare for his coming, as John the Baptist had. Jesus is building a movement through multiplying workers.
Question 2 ?	
Why do you think Jesus send out the seventy in pairs?	Two is the minimum number for there to be a witness to an event.[1]
	When two go out they can complement and encourage each other.
	When two strangers friendly with one another approach others, they can be less threatening than a lone individual.
Explanation ✓	Jesus' sending of the seventy in twos is also in alignment with Jesus' teaching in Matthew 18:19-20.
	"Again I say to you, that if two of you agree on earth about anything that they may ask, it shall be done for them by my Father who is in heaven. "For where two or three have gathered together in my name, I am there in their midst."

---

1. See Dt 17:6; 19:15; Mt 18:16; 2 Cor 13:1; 1 Tim 5:19.

Study Guide	Notes

Read Luke 10:2 📖

"And he was saying to them, "The harvest is plentiful, but the laborers are few; therefore beseech the Lord of the harvest to send out laborers into his harvest.""

Question 3 ?

What does Jesus tell the seventy here, and what how does that explain what he tells them to do?

Jesus tells the seventy that there is a plentiful harvest, but few laborers.

He asks them to beseech (beg), the Lord of the harvest to send out more laborers.

Explanation ✓

The word beseech means to beg, and the word "send out" (*ekballo*) means "to cast out." The seventy are asked to beg the Lord of the harvest to cast out workers, possibly because God prefers people go out willingly or are sent out deliberately by their communities.

Read Luke 10:3 📖

"Go; behold, I send you out as lambs in the midst of wolves."

Question 4 ?

To what does Jesus compare those he sends and why?

Jesus sends out his missionaries as lambs in the midst of wolves.

Explanation ✓

Jesus knowingly sends out his laborers out as vulnerable "lambs" into a harvest where they'll be surrounded by wolves, which prey on lambs. Jesus warns disciples that he's sending them out amidst dangerous predators.

Study Guide	Notes
Question 5 ?	
How and when might we encounter "wolves" when we go out in Jesus' name?	
Read Luke 10:4 📖	
"Carry no money belt, no bag, no shoes; and greet no one on the way."	
Question 6 ?	
What does Jesus tell his missionaries to not bring or do?	Those who Jesus sends are not to bring money, a bag, or shoes.
	They are not to greet anyone on the way.
Explanation ✓	Jesus' forerunners are instructed to deliberately go out in vulnerability, not depending on their own money or possessions.
	They are on a precise mission to go ahead of Jesus to the places where he will come. Their destinations are the homes of those who welcome them.
Read Luke 10:5-6 📖	
"Whatever house you enter, first say, 'Peace be to this house.' "If a man of peace is there, your peace will rest on him; but if not, it will return to you."	
Question 7 ?	
What's the first thing people to say when they arrive somewhere and with what result?	"Peace be to this home."
	If a person of peace is there the peace will rest on them. If not, it will return.

Study Guide	Notes

Explanation

When missionary disciples arrive at someone's house as strangers, people may be wary or resistant. Aware of this, Jesus advises his followers to speak peace over the household, which is something real and effective that we can offer to open the way into a home. If someone is receptive, open to them and their message, their peace will be received. If not, the peace will come back to us.

Read Luke 10:7-9

"Stay in that house, eating and drinking what they give you; for the laborer is worthy of his wages. Do not keep moving from house to house. "Whatever city you enter and they receive you, eat what is set before you; and heal those in it who are sick, and say to them, 'The Kingdom of God has come near to you.'

Question 8

What are Jesus' sent ones to do when they arrive at people's houses?

Those Jesus sent were to remain with their host family while in the place, receiving people's hospitality, eating and drinking what they serve.

They are also told to heal those who are sick and tell everyone: 'The Kingdom of God has come near to you.'

Study Guide	Notes

Explanation

Jesus literally tells his disciples: "You heal those in it who are sick." Jesus does not instruct those he sends to pray for God to heal, but to themselves heal with the authority he gives them. Jesus demonstrates healing in his many encounters in the Gospels. He never asks the Father to heal, but speaks words of healing (Mk 1:25) or instruction (Mt 8:13; 9:7; Lk 17:14), touches (Mt 8:3), invites people to receive and affirms people's faith. The Holy Spirit empowered Jesus' disciples in his physical absence to continue his mission the way he practiced it.

Read 10:10-12

"But whatever city you enter and they do not receive you, go out into its streets and say, 'Even the dust of your city which clings to our feet we wipe off in protest against you; yet be sure of this, that the Kingdom of God has come near.' "I say to you, it will be more tolerable in that day for Sodom than for that city."

Question 9

How are those Jesus sends out to respond when people do not receive them?

They are to go out into the streets of the city and publicly declare they are wiping the dust off their feet as a protest against the place.

They are to also declare that the Kingdom of God has come near to that city.

They are to state that the consequences for refusing them will be worse than what happened to Sodom.

Study Guide	Notes

Explanation

Refusal to receive those who God sends is strongly denounced throughout Scripture. Abraham and Sarah's hospitality to the Lord and two angels is contrasted to mistreatment by the people of Sodom in Genesis 18-19. In Luke 10:13-15 Jesus announces judgement against cities where he ministered:

"Woe to you, Chorazin! Woe to you, Bethsaida! For if the miracles had been performed in Tyre and Sidon which occurred in you, they would have repented long ago, sitting in sackcloth and ashes. "But it will be more tolerable for Tyre and Sidon in the judgment than for you. "And you, Capernaum, will not be exalted to heaven, will you? You will be brought down to Hades!" (10:13-15)

Read 10:16

"The one who listens to you listens to me, and the one who rejects you rejects me; and he who rejects me rejects the one who sent me."

Question 10

What does Jesus say about the people's response to those he sends?

Jesus equates those he sends with himself and his Father. The ones who receive or reject his missionaries, receive or reject Jesus and his Father.

Study Guide	Notes

Read 10:17-19

"The seventy returned with joy, saying, "Lord, even the demons are subject to us in your name." And he said to them, "I was watching Satan fall from heaven like lightning. "Behold, I have given you authority to tread on serpents and scorpions, and over all the power of the enemy, and nothing will injure you."

Question 11

What did the seventy report about their mission upon returning and how did Jesus respond?

The seventy returned with joy, telling Jesus that even demons were subject to them in his name.

Jesus told them he saw Satan fall from heaven like lightning. He adds that he's given them authority to step on snakes and scorpions, and over all the power of the enemy. He tells them "nothing will injure you."

Explanation

Serpents and scorpions are symbolic of predatory evil. In Genesis 1 God says of the human beings he's made in his image: "let them rule over the fish of the sea and over the birds of the sky and over the cattle and over all the earth, and over every creeping thing that creeps on the earth" (Gn 1:26).

God says to them: "Be fruitful and multiply, and fill the earth, and subdue it; and rule over the fish of the sea and over the birds of the sky and over every living thing that moves on the earth" (Gn 1:28).

Study Guide	Notes
Invitation ⟶	Ask people whether they are feeling drawn to step into the mission of the 70 here in Luke 10. Close in prayer, inviting people to affirm their desire, speaking out in their own words before God their interest in participating in Jesus' movement.

5.

JESUS LAUNCHES HIS MOVEMENT– KINGDOM OF GOD

MARK 3:7-15

Study Guide	Notes
Background	Mark's Gospel presents Jesus as beginning his ministry after his baptism. He goes to Galilee and preaches "the gospel of God," saying: "The time is fulfilled, and the Kingdom of God is at hand; repent and believe in the gospel"(Mk 1:15). Jesus then calls fishermen as disciples, teaches in the synagogue in Capernaum, and casts out an unclean spirit. Jesus heals Simon's mother-in-law of a fever. Then from her house he receives and heals crowds of sick people and casts out demons (1:32-33). He shows special care for the most marginalized, excluded people, cleansing a leper (1:40-44), publicly forgiving and healing a paralytic (2:1-12), calling Levi the tax collector as a disciple and eating with and defending sinners and tax collectors (2:14-17). Jesus' liberating actions on behalf of the most destitute (leper, paralytic) attract crowds (1:33, 45; 2:13). He defends his disciples before the Pharisees for picking and eating grain on the Sabbath, and openly defies them by publicly healing a man with a withered hand in the synagogue (Mk 3:1-5).
Introduction	In Mark 3:1-5 Jesus publicly challenges the religious leaders by breaking rules on behalf of people in need. We will see in the following study of Mark 3:6—how the religious leaders plot to destroy Jesus, and how Jesus withdraws into the marginal areas of Galilee, drawing people from all directions. Jesus increases his activity of healing, casting out demons and preaching; and he appoints his disciples to respond to the growing demands.

Study Guide	Notes

Read Mark 3:6

"The Pharisees went out and immediately began conspiring with the Herodians against him, as to how they might destroy him."

Question 1 ?

How did the Pharisees react to Jesus' healing the man with a withered hand in the synagogue on the Sabbath?

They went out and immediately plotted with the Herodians how to kill Jesus.

Explanation ✓

Mark presents the Pharisees as doing evil on the Sabbath, since Jesus had publicly asked them: "Is it lawful to do good or to do harm on the Sabbath, to save a life or to kill?" (Mk 3:4).

The Herodians were friends and partisans of Herod Antipas, the Jewish tetrarch of Galilee, and collaborator with the Roman Empire. Herod had imprisoned and beheaded John the Baptist (Mk 6:17). The Pharisees would have needed Herod's approval and help to do away with Jesus.

Read Mark 3:7-8

"Jesus withdrew to the sea with his disciples; and a great multitude from Galilee followed; and also from Judea, and from Jerusalem, and from Idumea, and beyond the Jordan, and the vicinity of Tyre and Sidon, a great number of people heard of all that he was doing and came to him."

Study Guide	Notes

Question 2 ?

Where did Jesus go and what did he do? How did people respond?

He retreated to the sea with his disciples.

Crowds followed him to important cities like Jerusalem, but mostly from outlying, marginalized places like Galilee, "beyond the Jordan" (East), and "Tyre and Sidon" (West and North) and "Idumea" (home of the Edomites in the Negev—South).

Great numbers of people heard all he was doing and came to him.

Explanation

Jesus retreated or withdrew, and Mark uses the Greek word *anachoreo*, which is often used in the Greek Old Testament to refer to military retreats during battle (Jo 8:15; Jdg 4:17; Jr 4:29). Jesus often retreated in response to persecution (Mt 4:12; 12:15; 14:13; 15:21; Jn 6:15).

Mark shows how Jesus' public healing of the man with a withered hand in the synagogue, where he broke the established Sabbath laws (according to the Pharisees) led religious leaders to plot with secular authorities to destroy him. When Jesus leaves the synagogue and retreats to the sea, crowds from Jerusalem and from non-Jewish places (North, South, East and West) are drawn to him. They saw Jesus as siding with them over and against the laws, offering freedom from diseases and problems they would tend to view as punishments.

The language here associates Jesus with Moses, who leaves Egypt for the Sea, together with a mixed multitude (Ex 12:38).

Study Guide	Notes

Read Mark 3:9-10 📖

"And he told his disciples that a boat should stand ready for him because of the crowd, so that they would not crowd him; for he had healed many, with the result that all those who had afflictions pressed around him in order to touch him."

Question 3 ?

What did Jesus tell the disciples to do and why?

Jesus told his disciples to get a boat ready so he could push off from the shore, getting some distance from the crowd of diseased people who sought to touch him and receive their healing.

People crowded Jesus because he healed many.

Explanation ✓

Direct contact with Jesus through people touching him (Mk 5:27, 28; 6:56) or him touching them (Mk 1:41; 7:33; 8:22; 10:13) is associated with healing throughout Mark.

Read Mark 3:11-12 📖

"Whenever the unclean spirits saw him, they would fall down before him and shout, "You are the Son of God!" And he earnestly warned them not to tell who he was."

Question 4 ?

What happened when unclean spirits saw Jesus and how did Jesus respond?

People with unclean spirits fell down before Jesus. The unclean spirits shouted out, identifying Jesus as the Son of God.

Jesus warned the unclean spirits to not tell anyone who he was.

Study Guide	Notes
Explanation ✓	This shows Jesus' authority over the unclean spirits.
Read Mark 3:13 📖 "And he went up on the mountain and summoned those whom he himself wanted, and they came to him."	
Question 5 ? What does Jesus do next and how did people respond?	He went up on a mountain and called to himself disciples he had chosen. Jesus' disciples came to him.
Explanation ✓	The disciples are described as coming to Jesus. But the words used here for "come to" (*aperchomai pros*) literally mean "went away to," "went off to," or "departed to" Jesus.
Read Mark 3:14-16 📖 "And he appointed twelve, so that they would be with him and that he could send them out to preach, and to have authority to cast out the demons. And he appointed the twelve."	
Question 6 ? What did Jesus do here?	Jesus appointed twelve disciples to be with him and so he could send them out to preach and cast out demons.

Study Guide	Notes
Explanation	Jesus literally "made twelve," rather than "appointed twelve," suggesting a creative act here.
	This verse links Jesus appointing of disciples to Moses' appointing of the 70 elders on the mountain in Numbers 11:25 and Exodus 24.
	Jesus intended to send out (*apostello*) his disciples to engage in the exact ministry he practiced from the outset in Mark 1:39 in Galilee when he was "preaching and casting out the demons."
Invitation	Take time to pray, telling Jesus about your efforts to follow him in his mission. Plan a time for a personal retreat for rest and spiritual refreshment with Jesus.

6.

JESUS SENDS OUT
THE TWELVE

MARK 6:1-14

Study Guide	Notes
Background	Mark's Gospel presents Jesus as beginning his ministry after his baptism. He goes to Galilee and preaches "the gospel of God:" The time is fulfilled, and the Kingdom of God is at hand; repent and believe in the gospel." Jesus then calls fishermen as disciples, teaches in the synagogue in Capernaum, and casts out an unclean spirit. Those witnessing Jesus are astonished by his authority. Jesus then receives hospitality from Simon's mother-in-law, who he heals of a fever. He stays in the house and heals all who come there, modeling the missional approach into which he commissions his disciples in Mark 6.
Introduction	In this story we see how Jesus teaches in the synagogue of his hometown, amazing and offending his fellow villagers. This keeps him from being able to do miracles there, and he is amazed by their unbelief. He goes from village to village, and sends out his disciples to do what he does in other villages.

Read Mark 6:1-2 📖

"Jesus went out from there and came into his hometown; and his disciples followed him. When the Sabbath came, he began to teach in the synagogue; and the many listeners were astonished, saying, "Where did this man get these things, and what is this wisdom given to him, and such miracles as these performed by his hands?"

Study Guide	Notes

Question 1

Where did Jesus go and what did he do? How did people respond?

He went with his disciples to his hometown and preached in the synagogue on the Sabbath.

Many listeners were astonished, asking where Jesus got "these things"—wisdom and miracles.

Explanation

The people wonder about the miracles Jesus performs with his hands—which they knew as the hands of a carpenter.

God's hand is associated with miracles. "And the hand of the Lord was with them, and a large number who believed turned to the Lord" (Acts 11:21).

Read Mark 6:3

"Is not this the carpenter, the son of Mary, and brother of James and Joses and Judas and Simon? Are not his sisters here with us?" And they took offense at him.'"

Question 2

How did the people of Jesus' hometown react to Jesus?

People asked questions about Jesus' identity—commenting that he was "the carpenter, the son of Mary. They mention his brothers by name and talked about how his sisters where there with them.

They took offence at him.

Study Guide	Notes

Explanation ✓

The people were literally scandalized by Jesus. *skandalizō* in Greek, which means "to put a stumbling-block or impediment in the way, upon which another may trip and fall; to be a stumbling-block; in the N.T. always metaphorically, (to cause or make to stumble; to offend (cause to offend).[1]

Question 3 ?

Why were people offended at Jesus? What would be the equivalent today?

The people were familiar with Jesus. They had ideas and judgments about who they thought he was, and couldn't accept that he was different or special.

Today people have a hard time believing someone can truly change or be different than they thought.

Read Mark 6:4-6 📖

"Jesus said to them, "A prophet is not without honor except in his hometown and among his own relatives and in his own household." And he could do no miracle there except that he laid his hands on a few sick people and healed them. And he wondered at their unbelief. And he was going around the villages teaching."

---

1. Thayer, *Thayer's Greek-English Lexicon*, 4624.

Study Guide	Notes
Question 4 ?	
How does Jesus explain his community's reaction? How did it affect his mission?	Jesus says that prophets are not without honor—except 1) In their hometown, 2) among their relatives, 3) in their own household.
	Jesus could do no miracle there. He could only lay his hands on a few people to heal them.
	He wondered at their unbelief.
	Jesus left to teach in other villages.
Explanation ✓	Jesus mentions three places where a prophet is without honor: homeland (*patris*), relatives (*yggenēs*) and household (*oikia*). These locations parallel locations Abraham was called to leave in response to God's call in Genesis 12:1 (LXX land (*gē*), relatives (*yggenēs*) and father's house (oukos – *tou patros*). Relatives are in the list of potential persecutors of believers (Lk 21:16).
	When Jesus' villagers take offence at him, he uses the occasion to teach his disciples about the obstacles to fruitful prophetic ministry: their homeland, relatives and immediate family. This teaching is present in every gospel (Mt 13:57; Lk 4:23; Jn 4:44) as a warning. If Jesus himself as God's Son scandalizes people who were familiar with him, who couldn't believe through him—how much more might this be the case for us! Jesus still wonders at the unbelief. But he keeps going, teaching in the surrounding villages rather than accepting minimal fruitfulness.

Study Guide	Notes
	Jesus increases his missional activity right at this point when he is rejected by his own, sending out his disciples to engage in his same actions.
Read Mark 6:7 📖 "And he summoned the twelve and began to send them out in pairs, and gave them authority over the unclean spirits."	
Question 5 ? What does Jesus do next?	He calls his twelve disciples and sends them out in pairs. He gave them authority over the unclean spirits—the same authority he used in the synagogue in Capernaum in his first miracle.
Explanation ✓	When Jesus calls his disciples a unique word is used, *proskaleo*, meaning "summon, call to." Jesus himself then sends them out, and the verb *apostello* is used, suggesting a commissioning and sending away on a special mission (Mt 10:5, 16; 11:10; 15:24; Mk 3:14; Lk 1:19; 4:18; Acts 10:20; Rm 10:15).
Question 6 ? Why do you think Jesus sent them out in pairs?	For greater security, companionship and complementary giftings.
Explanation ✓	Here Jesus gave his disciples authority over the unclean spirits. But the text doesn't give more details—like mentioning casting out demons or healing. Receiving authority over unclean spirits may include a wider governmental mandate over territory occupied by the powers.

Study Guide	Notes

Read Mark 6:8-9

"and he instructed them that they should take nothing for their journey, except a mere staff — no bread, no bag, no money in their belt — but to wear sandals; and He added, "Do not put on two tunics.""

Question 7

What does Jesus instruct his disciples to take and not to take?

Jesus instructs them to take nothing except a staff, but also to wear sandals.

He specifically instructs them to not take bread, a bag, or money.

Explanation

A staff (*rhabdos*) is a term designating a rod, staff but also a scepter—which a ruler would use to reign (See the Greek Version (Septuagint) of Ps 2:9; 44:6; 109:2; Isa 11:1; and Heb 1:8; Rev 2:27; 12:5; 19:15). The rod also has a prophetic function in the OT, as when Moses performs signs of judgment before Pharaoh, seeking the liberation from slavery of God's people (Ex 4:2-5; 7:9-10, 12, 17, 19; 8:5, 16; 10:13) and to signs to confirm prophetic words (Jdg 6:21). The staff is used to accomplish miracles of liberation (Ex 14:16; 17:19), and as a symbol of shepherding God's people (LXX Ps 22:4; Mi 7:14).

Wearing sandals associates Jesus' sending out with the exodus, when on the eve of the Israelite slaves departure from Egypt God instructed them: "Now in this way you shall eat it: your loins girded and your sandals on your feet and your staves in your hands. And you shall eat it with haste—it is the Lord's Passover" (Ex 12:11 LXX)

Study Guide	Notes

Read the following texts about the staff 📖

"Thy throne O God, is for ever and ever: the scepter of thy kingdom is a scepter of righteousness" (Ps 44:6 LXX).

"A rod of your power the Lord will send out from Sion. And exercise dominion in the midst of your enemies!" (Ps 109:2 LXX).

"And you, raise your rod, and stretch out your hand over the sea, and break it apart, and let the sons of Israel enter into the midst of the sea on what was dry" (Ex 14:16 LXX).

"Shepherd your people with your rod, the sheep of your possession" (Mi 7:14 LXX).

Question 9   ?

What do you think carrying a staff and wearing sandals signify based on these texts? How might these items change the way disciples see themselves and their mission?

Question 10   ?

Why do you think Jesus tells his disciples not to take bread, a bag or money, and to not put on two tunics?

He wanted disciples to go in vulnerability, dependent on God and their hosts.

Read Mark 6:10 📖

"And he said to them, "Wherever you enter a house, stay there until you leave town.""

Study Guide	Notes

Question 11   ?

What are disciples to do when they enter a house? Why?

Keep staying in the same house that welcomes you until you leave town.

Jesus is inviting disciples to receive hospitality and provision from local people, to build relationships and possibly establish the household as a future faith community.

Read Mark 6:11   📖

"Any place that does not receive you or listen to you, as you go out from there, shake the dust off the soles of your feet for a testimony against them."

Question 12   ?

What does Jesus tell his disciples here and why?

Disciples are to shake off the dust from the soles of their feet of those who do not receive them or listen. This is a testimony against them. But it could also signify the importance of ridding themselves of the traces of rejection that could lead to discouragement.

Read Mark 6:12-13   📖

"They went out and preached that men should repent. And they were casting out many demons and were anointing with oil many sick people and healing them."

Question 13   ?

What do the disciples do when they go out?

They preached that people should repent.

They were casting our many demons.

They were anointing with oil many sick people and healing them.

Study Guide	Notes
Explanation	In this text Jesus does not send the disciples out to preach, cast out demons and heal the sick. Jesus had only given his disciples authority over unclean spirits, which the disciples freely interpreted as including these activities, which often appear together (Mt 10:7-8; Lk 9:1-2).
	There is little mention of this practice of anointing people with oil in the gospels, though this practice is mentioned in James 5:14. "Is anyone among you sick? *Then* he must call for the elders of the church and they are to pray over him, anointing him with oil in the name of the Lord."
Invitation ⟶	Do you see a need to receive authority from Jesus over unclean spirits, to preach that people should repent, to cast out demons and heal the sick? Take a moment to express your desire to receive authority from Jesus over unclean spirits. Ask Jesus to send you out on missions to advance his kingdom.
	Ask the Holy Spirit to show you personally if your need to change your way of thinking about God or yourself (repentance), or if there are any demons that you must send away or healing that you yourself need now. Take a moment to pray.

| **Study Guide** | **Notes** |

Read Mark 6:14

"And King Herod heard of it, for his name had become well known; and people were saying, "John the Baptist has risen from the dead, and that is why these miraculous powers are at work in him.""

Explanation

Notice that the local political authority, King Herod heard about Jesus' movement. He immediately wonders whether John the Baptist whom he'd beheaded had risen from the dead. Jesus and his disciples' activity of advancing the Kingdom of God threatens the established powers. The next verses tell how Herod had arrested, imprisoned and executed John the Baptist for his prophetic denunciation of taking his brother's wife.

Read Mark 6:30-32

"The apostles gathered together with Jesus; and they reported to him all that they had done and taught. And he said to them, "Come away by yourselves to a secluded place and rest a while." (For there were many people coming and going, and they did not even have time to eat.) They went away in the boat to a secluded place by themselves."

Study Guide	Notes
Question 14 ?	They are called apostles.
What happens once Jesus' disciples return from their mission?	They gather together with Jesus.
	They report to him everything they'd both done and taught.
	Jesus invites them to come away with just him to a secluded place to rest.
	Many people were coming and going and they didn't even have time to eat.
	They all went away in a boat to a secluded place for a retreat.
Invitation ⟶	Take time to pray, telling Jesus about your efforts to follow him in his mission. Plan a time for a personal retreat for rest and spiritual refreshment with Jesus.

7.

JESUS HEALS A WOMAN AND A YOUNG GIRL

LUKE 8:4-56

Study Guide	Notes
Background	Jesus has just returned from the country of the Gerasenes on the far side of the lake (Lk 8:26). There, a violent demoniac who was living in the tombs fell before Jesus and cried out to him for mercy (Lk 8:27–29). Jesus cast the demons out of the man and into a herd of two thousand pigs, which destroyed the wealthy herdsmen's business and led the locals to drive him out of town (Lk 8:30–34). Then Jesus commissioned the newly liberated man to bear witness about God had done for him to his household and region (Lk 8:39).

In today's story, another man falls down before Jesus and begs him for mercy because the man's young daughter is dying. |
| **Read Luke 8:40–42** 📖 | |
| "And as Jesus returned, the people welcomed him, for they had all been waiting for him. And there came a man named Jairus, and he was an official of the synagogue; and he fell at Jesus'feet, and began to implore him to come to his house; for he had an only daughter, about twelve years old, and she was dying. But as he went, the crowds were pressing against him." | |

Study Guide	Notes

Question 1   ?

What is happening in this story? Who comes to Jesus and why?

Jesus returns from his mission across the lake.

A synagogue official named Jairus comes to Jesus, falls down at his feet, and begs him to come to his house because his only daughter, who is twelve, is dying.

As Jesus goes with Jairus, the crowd presses against him.

Explanation   ✓

Here, Jairus publicly falls at Jesus' feet and begs him to come to his house.

In other Gospel stories, we see others fall down before Jesus : a leper falls on his face before Jesus and begs him for healing (Lk 5:12); a Samaritan leper falls on his face at Jesus' feet and thanks him for healing him (Lk 17:16); Mary falls at Jesus' feet, lamenting the death of her brother, Lazarus (Jn 11:32).

Falling (*pipto*) is an act of humble surrender before someone, such as when a slave falls before a master (see Mt 18:26, 29), or when Jesus falls on his face before his Father (Mt 26:39).

Read Luke 8:43–44   📖

"And a woman who had a hemorrhage for twelve years, and could not be healed by anyone, came up behind him and touched the fringe of his cloak, and immediately her hemorrhage stopped."

Study Guide	Notes
Question 2 ? Now who comes to Jesus? What do we know about this woman? What does she do and what happens to her?	A woman who has been bleeding for twelve years. She cannot be healed by anyone. She comes up behind Jesus and touches the fringe of his cloak. Immediately her bleeding stops.
Question 3 ? How is the woman's approach to Jesus different from Jairus's?	The woman is probably poor, as she has spent everything on doctors. The woman is nameless, whereas Jairus is named. The woman herself is afflicted, whereas Jairus comes to Jesus and risks his reputation because he loves his dying daughter. The woman comes up secretly behind Jesus in the crowd and touches the fringe of his garment, whereas Jairus approaches Jesus in front of a huge crowd. She is immediately healed, whereas Jairus has to wait to see what will happen to his daughter.

Read Luke 8:45–46 📖

"And Jesus said, 'Who is the one who touched me?' And while they were all denying it, Peter said, 'Master, the people are crowding and pressing in on you.' But Jesus said, 'Someone did touch me, for I was aware that power had gone out of me.'"

Study Guide	Notes

Question 4

How does Jesus respond and why?

Jesus asks, "who touched me?"

He is aware that power has gone out of him.

Question 5

Why do you think Jesus asks this question?

Does he want a more personal encounter with this person who has touched him?

He wants to address this person in a way that brings further healing and empowerment.

Explanation

God speaks to someone outside the system, someone on the margins (in the wilderness). God's order of preference is different (see the Magnificat in Lk 1:52).

Read Luke 8:47–48

"When the woman saw that she had not escaped notice, she came trembling and fell down before him, and declared in the presence of all the people the reason why she had touched him, and how she had been immediately healed. And he said to her, 'Daughter, your faith has made you well; go in peace.'"

Study Guide	Notes

Question 6   ?

How does the woman respond to Jesus' question?

When the woman realizes that Jesus noticed how she touched him, she falls down trembling before him and declares her secret and her prior physical condition before all the people.

The word "fall" (*prospipto*) means "to prostrate oneself before someone, implying supplication—'to fall down before.'"

The woman declares how she was immediately healed after touching Jesus.

The woman becomes a witness to her people, similar to the Gerasene demoniac after his deliverance (Lk 8:39).

Question 7   ?

How does Jesus respond to the woman?

Why does Jesus call her daughter?

Jesus calls her daughter, filling the role of a father. He acts as the woman's advocate, which she has not had during her twelve-year illness.

Jesus publicly gives her credit for the healing, saying, "your faith has made you well."

Jesus sends her away in peace, freeing her from her shame.

Read Luke 8:49–50   📖

"While he was still speaking, someone came from the house of the synagogue official, saying, 'Your daughter has died; do not trouble the Teacher anymore.' But when Jesus heard this, he answered him, 'Do not be afraid any longer; only believe, and she will be made well.'"

Study Guide	Notes
Question 8 ?	
What news comes next? How does Jesus respond?	Right after the woman is healed and dismissed by Jesus, a messenger from Jairus's house announces bad news: "your daughter has died; don't trouble the teacher anymore."
	Jesus hears and encourages him not to be afraid, but to believe that she'll be made well.
Read Luke 8:51 📖	
"When he came to the house, he did not allow anyone to enter with him, except Peter and John and James, and the girl's father and mother."	
Question 9 ?	
Why do you think Jesus only allows select people to enter Jairus's house with him?"	Jesus continues on his way to Jairus's house and leaves the crowd outside, respecting the grief of Jairus and his family.
	He brings his closest disciples with him. They have just witnessed the bleeding woman's healing, and so he brings them as witnesses and also to increase their faith.
Read Luke 8:52–53 📖	
"Now they were all weeping and lamenting for her; but he said, 'Stop weeping, for she has not died, but is asleep.' And they began laughing at him, knowing that she had died."	

Study Guide	Notes

Question 10   ?

What is happening in the house? How does Jesus respond? How do the people respond to Jesus?

Everyone is crying and grieving over the little girl.

Jesus tells them to stop crying because she has not died but is sleeping.

The people laugh at (or mock) Jesus.

Read Luke 8:54–56   📖

"He, however, took her by the hand and called, saying, 'Child, arise!' And her spirit returned, and she got up immediately; and he gave orders for something to be given her to eat. Her parents were amazed; but he instructed them to tell no one what had happened."

Question 11   ?

What does Jesus do next? What instructions does he give?

Jesus takes the girl by the hand. He calls to her, saying, "Child arise!"

In Mark's account, Jesus says to her, "*Talitha kum*!" which means, "Little girl, I say to you, get up!" (Mk 5:41).

Immediately she gets up and Jesus tells people to give her something to eat.

Her parents are amazed, but Jesus tells them not to tell anyone what has happened.

Question 12   ?

How is this story of healing different from the previous story about the bleeding woman?

Here, Jesus takes the initiative to touch the little girl (he takes her by the hand) and speak to her. His communication with her is private rather than public.

Moreover, Jesus instructs the witnesses not to tell anyone what has happened.

Study Guide	Notes

Question 13

What does this story tell us about how we can make contact with Jesus and how he might respond?

All people can freely come to Jesus, from important officials to chronically ill women filled with shame.

Jesus is present wherever people are in need. He is available and can be approached publicly or privately.

Jesus responds effectively to people's needs and brings healing.

He uses a unique approach with each person who comes to him, pursuing relationship rather than simply fixing the problem miraculously.

Jesus brings dignity, hope, and empowerment to those he helps.

Invitation ———>

Do you feel drawn to Jesus as he reveals himself in these stories?

Do you need Jesus to help you with any personal problems?

Invite people to tell Jesus how they feel drawn to him and how they desire to follow him.

Invite people to draw near to Jesus in prayer, sharing their needs silently or out loud.

8.

JESUS LIBERATES AN OPPRESSED BOY

MARK 9:14-29

Study Guide	Notes

Background

Prior to this story, Jesus takes Peter, James, and John to the top of a high mountain by themselves, where he is transfigured. Elijah and Moses appear and talk with Jesus, and Peter, James, and John are terrified. As they come down the mountain, Jesus gives them orders not to tell anyone what they had seen.

Introduction

In this story, we see Jesus' last public miracle, which involves casting out an evil spirit from a boy. In Jesus' first miracle (Mk 1:23–27), he rebukes an unclean spirit from someone in the synagogue. Later, Jesus brings his disciples with him to free the Gerasene demoniac from a legion of demons (Mk 5:1–20). Then he commissions his disciples to cast out unclean spirits (Mk 6:7, 13). Here, Jesus shows his disciples and all who follow him that those who are suffering from lifelong afflictions can be liberated.

Read Mark 9:14–18   📖

"When they came back to the disciples, they saw a large crowd around them, and some scribes arguing with them. Immediately, when the entire crowd saw him, they were amazed and began running up to greet him. And he asked them, 'What are you discussing with them?' And one of the crowd answered him, 'Teacher, I brought you my son, possessed with a spirit which makes him mute; and whenever it seizes him, it slams him to the ground and he foams at the mouth, and grinds his teeth and stiffens out. I told your disciples to cast it out, and they could not do it.'"

Study Guide	Notes
Question 1 ?	
What happens after Jesus comes back with Peter, James, and John to the rest of his disciples?	There is a large crowd gathered around his disciples, and some scribes are arguing with them. Jesus asks them what they are discussing, and a man tells him how he brought his son, who was afflicted by an evil spirit, to the disciples, but they couldn't cast it out.
Question 2 ?	
What was wrong with the man's son?	The boy has an evil spirit that makes him unable to speak, which is an opposite action to the Holy Spirit that emboldens and empowers people to bear witness (Mk 13:11).
	The spirit seizes the boy and slams him to the ground, where he foams at the mouth, grinds his teeth, and stiffens out.
Question 3 ?	
Do you see or experience these kinds of symptoms today?	Invite people to share their disappointments and ongoing needs for breakthrough.
Question 4 ?	
Have you ever brought someone with big problems to Jesus' followers (Christians, the church) and not received the help you hoped for?	Invite people to share any relevant experiences of not receiving healing or freedom from the church or from God.
	Another possible question is: has anyone come to you with a difficult problem that you pray for, but see no response?
	Let's look at how Jesus responds.

Study Guide	Notes

Read Mark 9:19 📖

"And he answered them and said, 'O unbelieving generation, how long shall I be with you? How long shall I put up with you? Bring him to me!'"

Question 5 ?

How does Jesus react?

Jesus seems frustrated. He calls all the people the "unbelieving generation."

He seems to expect his disciples and the people themselves to be able to cast out evil spirits and experience freedom.

Jesus wonders how much longer he must be with people to equip and empower them to exercise their faith and authority as he does.

The failure of Jesus' disciples does not mean there's no hope for freedom. Jesus tells the man to bring his son directly to him.

Explanation ✓

Jesus includes everyone in his critique—his disciples and the people. Throughout Mark's Gospel, Jesus highlights the importance of believing. When Jesus returns from the wilderness, he says, "Repent and believe in the gospel" (Mk 1:15). He tells the synagogue official whose daughter has just died, "do not be afraid any longer, only believe" (Mk 5:36).

After the resurrection, when Jesus appears to his disciples as they are eating, he says, "The one who believes and has been baptized shall be saved. . . These signs will accompany those who have believed: in my name they will cast out demons" (Mk 16:16–17).

Study Guide	Notes
Invitation ———▷	Are there chronic problems that the church or Christians haven't been able to help you with? Do you want to bring those directly to Jesus now?
	Invite people to bring their ongoing concerns to Jesus in prayer.

Read Mark 9:20 📖

"They brought the boy to him. When he saw him, immediately the spirit threw him into a convulsion, and falling to the ground, he began rolling around and foaming at the mouth."

Question 6 ❓

What happens when they bring the boy to Jesus?	The evil spirit throws the boy into a convulsion as soon as either the boy sees Jesus or Jesus sees the boy (it is impossible to tell to whom "he saw" refers).
	Bringing the boy to Jesus and "seeing" is presented here as a confrontation that provokes a reaction from the spirit, which then tries to destroy the boy.
	There is not immediate and automatic deliverance in Jesus' presence. Further action is needed that includes the father.
Explanation ✓	When people are brought to Jesus or come to Jesus with a problem, things can get worse before they get better. The worsening of a person's condition can discourage people, and the evil spirit wants to intimidate everyone by demonstrating its power in order to make them feel powerless and lose faith.
	Let's see how Jesus responds.

Study Guide	Notes

Read Mark 9:21–22 📖

"And he asked his father, 'How long has this been happening to him?' And he said, 'From childhood. It has often thrown him both into the fire and into the water to destroy him. But if you can do anything, take pity on us and help us!'"

Question 7 ?

Why does Jesus ask, "how long has this been happening"?

Jesus asks the father about the duration of his son's suffering—or the history of the problem.

Question 8 ?

How does the father respond?

The father answers that his son has been suffering since childhood. Then he offers more details about how the evil spirit has tried to kill his son by throwing him into the water and the fire.

The father shows his discouragement and desperation, but also his weakened faith when he says: "*If* you can do anything, take pity on us and help us."

The father may wonder if Jesus can resolve his son's chronic problem, since the boy wasn't immediately delivered.

Study Guide	Notes
Explanation ✓	The boy's father cries out in desperate intercession: "Have compassion on us! Help us!"
	In Mark's Gospel, Jesus' compassion leads to healing (Mk 1:41), teaching (Mk 6:34), and feeding (Mk 8:2).
	The father's cry for Jesus to "help us" uses the same term (*boetheo*) as the Greek version of Israel's prayers in the psalms (See Ps 40:13 [LXX Ps 39:13]; 44:26 [LXX 43:26]; 70:5 [LXX 69:5]; 79:9 [LXX 78:9]; 109:26 [LXX 108:26]; 119:86 [LXX 118:86], 119:117 [LXX 118:117]).
	Mark's account helps readers relate this situation to their own chronic, unsolvable problems, inviting hope.
Read Mark 9:23–24 📖	
"And Jesus said to him, 'If you can?' All things are possible to him who believes. Immediately the boy's father cried out and said, 'I do believe; help my unbelief.'"	
Question 9 ?	
What exactly does Jesus say to the father here, and how does the father respond?	Jesus asks him a question in a way that directly challenges his unbelief: "*If you can?*"
	Jesus boldly says, "All things are possible to him who believes" (literally, "to the one who is believing).
	The boy's father cries out immediately, stating his faith and asking Jesus to help his unbelief.
	Other passages in Mark also use the phrase, "cry out" (Mk 5:7; 10:47).

Study Guide	Notes

Explanation

Jesus insists that believing is essential. In Mark 11:23, he states, "whoever says to this mountain, 'Be taken up and cast into the sea,' and does not doubt in his heart, but believes that what he says is going to happen, it will be granted him."

Read Mark 9:25

"When Jesus saw that a crowd was rapidly gathering, he rebuked the unclean spirit, saying to it, 'You deaf and mute spirit, I command you, come out of him and do not enter him again.'"

Question 10

What happens next and what does Jesus do?

The crowd gathers rapidly, so Jesus acts quickly.

Jesus rebukes the "unclean spirit" (this is the first time it is described in this way).

He speaks to it directly: "You deaf and dumb spirit . . ."

He exercises authority over it, commanding it with precise instructions: "come out of him and don't enter him again," which suggests that spirits can come back.

Study Guide	Notes
Question 11 ?	
What does this tell us about Jesus and God, since Jesus reveals God?	Jesus represents "the one who believes," for whom anything is possible (even freeing a boy who has been oppressed since childhood).
	He is antagonistic towards unclean spirits.
	He has authority over these spirits.
	He names the spirits precisely and gives them precise instructions.
	He cares about the boy and acts quickly to avoid a public scene.
	He communicates with people who have little faith.
	He wants his disciples (and us) to learn from him.
Read Mark 9:26–27 📖	
"After crying out and throwing him into terrible convulsions, it came out; and the boy became so much like a corpse that most of them said, 'He is dead!' But Jesus took him by the hand and raised him; and he got up."	
Question 12 ?	
What happens next and how does Jesus respond?	The unclean spirit cries out and throws the boy into convulsions before coming out.
	The boy is like a corpse and people say he's dead.
	Jesus takes him by the hand and raises him up.
	The boy gets up.

Study Guide	**Notes**

Read Mark 9:28–29 📖

"When he came into the house, his disciples began questioning him privately, 'Why could we not drive it out?' And he said to them, 'This kind cannot come out by anything but prayer.'"

Question 13 ?

What do the disciples say to Jesus about this miracle and what does he teach them?

The disciples want to know why they couldn't cast out the unclean spirit from the boy. After all, they had been prepared and were successful earlier (see Mk 6:7, 13).

Jesus tells them that casting out this kind of spirit requires prayer. (In Mt 17, Jesus says that faith, prayer, and fasting are necessary.)

Consider Reading 📖
Matthew 17:20–21

"And he said to them, 'Because of the littleness of your faith; for truly I say to you, if you have faith the size of a mustard seed, you will say to this mountain, "Move from here to there," and it will move; and nothing will be impossible to you. But this kind does not go out except by prayer and fasting.'"

Study Guide	Notes

Explanation

Jesus teaches his disciples that prayer is necessary in order see breakthrough when casting out unclean spirits in more difficult cases.

The father himself is modeling prayer in his communication with Jesus (God). He brings his son to Jesus and cries out for compassion and help. He affirms his belief and confesses his unbelief. Jesus frees his son.

When the disciples come to Jesus and ask him a question, this is also prayer.

Jesus does not pray to God to cast out the unclean spirit, but rather he himself names the spirit and orders it to go out and not return. Jesus instructs his disciples to cast out unclean spirits, not to pray for God to cast them out. Prayer strengthens disciples in their authority and effectiveness as they put into practice what the Holy Spirit indicates.

Invitation

Consider an area in your life where you need a miracle. Confess any unbelief you have and ask Jesus to help you believe. Consider if God is asking you to exercise your own authority in any particular way.

9.

THE RESURRECTED JESUS MEETS AND COMMISSIONS HIS DISCIPLES

MARK 13:1-20

Study Guide	Notes
Introduction	In the Gospel of Mark's account of Jesus' resurrection, a young man at the empty tomb tells women bringing spices to the tomb that Jesus has risen and is not there. He tells the women to tell Jesus' disciples that he will meet them in Galilee. The women flee the tomb, trembling and astonished. The most ancient manuscripts end Mark's Gospel at Mk 16:8. In the longer ending (Mk 16:9-19) Jesus appears to select disciples, but the others do not believe. Finally he meets up with the eleven disciples, challenging them regarding their unbelief, and sending them to continue his movement throughout the world.
Suggestion	Mark's Gospel has several endings, with the oldest manuscripts ending after Mark 16:8. This Bible study focusses on the longer ending, Mark 16:9-19. If there is time to read it is best to read Mark 16:1-8 and discuss the first two questions below as part of a longer Bible study that ends with Mark 16:19. If there's not time, you can either 1) break this study into two separate studies (Mk 16:1-8 and Mk 16:9-19), or 2) briefly summarize Mark 16:1-8 and then begin reading at Mark 16:9 and discuss beginning at question 3 below.

Study Guide	Notes

Read Mark 16:1-5

"When the Sabbath was over, Mary Magdalene, and Mary the mother of James, and Salome, bought spices, so that they might come and anoint him. Very early on the first day of the week, they came to the tomb when the sun had risen. They were saying to one another, "Who will roll away the stone for us from the entrance of the tomb?" Looking up, they saw that the stone had been rolled away, although it was extremely large. Entering the tomb, they saw a young man sitting at the right, wearing a white robe; and they were amazed."

Question 1

What happens in these verses?

Two women, Mary Magdalene and another Mary go to the tomb early in the morning on the first day of the week to anoint Jesus' body.

They ask themselves "who will roll away the stone from the tomb entrance?" But when they arrive they find the extremely large stone has been rolled away.

They enter the tomb and encounter a young man dressed in white and they are amazed.

Study Guide	Notes
Explanation	The Greek verb here for amazement is *ekthambeō*, which means 1) "to throw into amazement or terror; to alarm thoroughly, to terrify: or 2) to be struck with amazement; to be thoroughly amazed, astounded."[1] It occurs only here and in two other places in Mark's Gospel in the entire New Testament (see Mark 9:15; 14:33). In Mark 14:33 it is best translated as "distressed," and is paralleled with "troubled."

Read Mark 16:6-7

"And he said to them, 'Do not be amazed; you are looking for Jesus the Nazarene, who has been crucified. He has risen; he is not here; behold, here is the place where they laid him. 'But go, tell his disciples and Peter, 'he is going ahead of you to Galilee; there you will see him, just as he told you.'"

Question 2

Why did the young man tell them: "do not be amazed (or terrified)?"

Question 3

What did the man tell them in response to their amazement, or terror? Why would he tell them these things?	He told them that Jesus has been raised and they can look and see that he is not there.
	He tells them to tell Jesus' disciples and Peter, and that he's going ahead of them to Galilee where they will see him as he told them.

---

1. Thayer, *Thayer's Greek-English Lexicon*, 1568.

Study Guide	Notes

Read Mark 16:8 📖

"They went out and fled from the tomb, for trembling and astonishment had gripped them; and they said nothing to anyone, for they were afraid."

Question 4 ?

What do the women do?

They go out and flee from the tomb, trembling and astonished.

They say nothing to anyone, because they are afraid.

Explanation ✓

In Mark's Gospel the first witnesses of the resurrection are described as reacting with precise language:

"They <u>went out</u> [of the tomb] and <u>fled</u>, for <u>trembling</u> and <u>astonishment</u> had <u>gripped</u> them."

Fleeing (*pheugō*) is presented negatively in Mark's Gospel (Mk 5:14; 14:50).

Trembling (*tromos*) can mean "quaking with fear." It only occurs here in the Gospels, but is present in Paul's writings (1 Cor 2:3; 2 Cor 7:15; Eph 6:5; Phil 2:12).

Astonishment (*ekstasis*), "displacement of mind, bewilderment, amazement, trance" only occurs in Mark's Gospel in 5:42, when Jesus raises Jairus' 12-year-old daughter from the dead. It occurs elsewhere in response to miracles (Lk 5:26; Acts 3:10) and in descriptions of trances (Acts 10:10; 11:5; 22:17).

Literally this says: "trembling and astonishment had them."

Study Guide	Notes

Question 5 ?

Do you or people you know ever respond to challenges by escaping or disassociating? How? Why?

People escape troubling life situations through addictions, entertainment, busyness, exercise, travel, etc.

Explanation ✓

In Mark's Gospel and elsewhere in the New Testament the Greek verb translated "afraid" (*phobeō*) means both 1) "to terrify, frighten, (Mk 4:41; 5:33; 6:50; 10:32; 11:18,32; Lk 8:50; 12:7,32; Jn 12:15; 19:8; Acts 16:38; 22:29; Rom 13:4; Heb 13:6; 1 Jn 4:18), and 2) "to reverence, venerate, to treat with deference or reverential obedience" (Mk 5:15, 36; 6:20; 9:6; Eph 5:33; Lk 1:50; 18:2, 4; Acts 10:2, 22, 35; Col 3:22; 1 Pt 2:17; Rv 14:7; 19:5).[2] Daniel Bourguet comments: "They said nothing to anyone because they were gripped by holy fear." To translate this final verse in this way is altogether within the logic of this gospel, directed as it is towards contemplation; this all leads to the thought that the women found themselves before such a mystery that it overturned the fear that caused them to flee, turning it into the awe that reduced them to silence."[3]

Question 6 ?

With this original ending of the Gospel of Mark highlighting the trembling and awestruck women witnesses, how could you imagine the Jesus movement advancing?

---

2. Thayer, *Thayer's Greek-English Lexicon*, 5399.

3. Daniel Bourguet, *The Humble Divinity of Jesus in Mark's Gospel*, Volume 2, Translated by Roger Wilkinson, Burlington: The People's Seminary Press, 2021, p. 139.

Study Guide	Notes

Read Mark 16:9-11

"Now after he had risen early on the first day of the week, he first appeared to Mary Magdalene, from whom he had cast out seven demons. She went and reported to those who had been with him, while they were mourning and weeping. When they heard that he was alive and had been seen by her, they refused to believe it."

Question 7

To whom does Jesus appear and how do they respond?

The resurrected Jesus appears to Mary Magdalene, who the young man had previously spoken to at the tomb. Mark notes that Jesus had cast out seven demons from her.

She reported it to those who had been with Jesus, who were mourning and weeping.

They refused to believe that he was alive and that she'd seen him.

Question 8

Do you have any personal experience with demons or know anyone who does? How would people view someone who had come from a hard background like Mary?

Study Guide	Notes

Question 9

What does the choice of these first messengers tell us about the kinds of people God chooses to bear witness?

A young man dressed is white, sitting at the right in the tomb is the first messenger.

The young man appears to two women, commissioning them to tell the good news that Jesus is alive to the male disciples

Jesus himself appears to a woman with a difficult past, formally afflicted by seven demons, to tell Jesus' mourning disciples that he was alive.

Read Mark 16:12-13

"After that, he appeared in a different form to two of them while they were walking along on their way to the country. They went away and reported it to the others, but they did not believe them either."

Question 10 ?

To whom does Jesus appear and how do they respond?

Jesus appeared to two people who were walking in the country. They went and told it to the others.

The others didn't believe them either.

Study Guide	Notes
Explanation	Jesus is not mentioned by name here, but just as "he."
	He "appears" in a different form to two unnamed disciples while they were walking to the country.
	The two "report" (*apangellō*) to the eleven the details of the resurrected Jesus' appearance and words to them. "Reporting" is a reporting of what witnesses have themselves seen or heard (see Mt 8:33; 11:4; 14:12; 28:8, 10; Mk 5:14, 19; 6:30; 16:10; Lk 7:18, 22).
Question 11	
What does this tell us about Jesus that he keeps trying to communicate with people who don't believe?	Jesus is faithful, even though humans can be faithless.
	Unbelief does not disqualify us.
	Jesus believes in us, despite our unbelief in him.
Read Mark 16:14	
"Afterward he appeared to the eleven themselves as they were reclining at the table; and he reproached them for their unbelief and hardness of heart, because they had not believed those who had seen him after he had risen."	
Question 12	
What did Jesus do and say here to the eleven disciples? What does that tell us about Jesus?	Jesus appeared to the eleven disciples while they were having a meal. He reproached them for their unbelief and hardness of heart—because they hadn't believed those who had seen him after he'd resurrected.
	Jesus believes in his disciples and doesn't give up on them, despite their unbelief and hardness of heart.

Study Guide	Notes

Explanation

Jesus reproached (*oneidizo*) his disciples, meaning "to insult, to reproach someone, with the implication of that individual being evidently to blame — to reprimand."

Unbelief (*apistia*) is mentioned often in the Gospels. It kept Jesus from doing many miracles in his hometown (Mt 13:58). In Mark's Gospel Jesus wondered at people's unbelief (Mk 6:6), which was confessed by the father of a demonized boy (Mk 9:24). Paul says God's people were broken off due to their unbelief (Rm 11:20), and can be grafted back in if they do not remain in unbelief (Rm 11:23). An "unbelieving heart" causes someone to "fall away from the living God" (Hb 3:12) and not enter God's rest (3:19).

Hardness of heart (*sklerokardia*) means "pertaining to being obdurate and obstinate — 'stubborn, completely unyielding.'"[4] This same term appears in the Greek Old Testament in texts about Israel being stiff-necked, and consequently not entering the promised land (Ex 33:3, 4; 34:9), but that God saved them all the same (Dt 9:6, 13).

Question 13

Why was Jesus especially upset with the eleven?

Because they had not believed those who had seen Jesus.

---

4. Louw and Nida, *Greek-English Lexicon*, 88.224.

Study Guide	Notes
Explanation ✓	Believing (*pisteuō*) is especially important in Mark's Gospel. Jesus tells his disciples: "The time is fulfilled, and the Kingdom of God is at hand; repent and believe in the gospel" (Mk 1:15).
	Jesus tells the synagogue official whose daughter has just died: "Do not be afraid *any longer*, only believe" (Mk 5:36), and the man with the demonized boy: "All things are possible to him who believes" (Mk 9:23).
	He also says:
	"Truly I say to you, whoever says to this mountain, 'Be taken up and cast into the sea,' and does not doubt in his heart, but believes that what he says is going to happen, it will be granted him" (Mk 11:23).
	"All things for which you pray and ask, believe that you have received them, and they will be granted you" (Mk 11:24).
Question 14 ?	
Do you see unbelief and hardness of heart in followers of Jesus today (or in yourself)?	
Invitation ⟶	Invite people to confess unbelief and hardness of heart before God and each other. Remind people that Jesus forgives us for our sins.
Read Mark 16:15 📖	
"And he said to them, "Go into all the world and preach the gospel to all creation."	

Study Guide	Notes
Question 15 ?	
What does Jesus say to the eleven who he has just reproached?	Jesus sends out his disciples to preach the gospel to all creation, despite having just reproached them for their unbelief and hardness of heart.
Read Mark 16:16 📖	
"He who has believed and has been baptized shall be saved; but he who has disbelieved shall be condemned."	
Question 16 ?	
What does Jesus say here, and what do you think he means?	Whoever believes the gospel and is baptized will be saved.
	The one who doesn't believe will be condemned.
	Jesus emphasizes the importance of believe the good news so as to be saved and not condemned.
Explanation ✓	Believing in Jesus and being baptized brings salvation, while the one who disbelieves will be condemned.
	Notice that it doesn't say <u>who</u> will condemned the unbelieving.
Question 17 ?	
What is associated here with those have believed?	Baptism and salvation.

Study Guide	Notes

Read Mark 16:17-18

"These signs will accompany those who have believed: in my name they will cast out demons, they will speak with new tongues; they will pick up serpents, and if they drink any deadly poison, it will not hurt them; they will lay hands on the sick, and they will recover."

Question 18

What does Jesus say here at the very beginning of Mark 16:17?

Explanation

"These signs will accompany those who have believed: in my name they will…"

"These signs will accompany" comes from two words "signs" (*sēmeion*), and "accompany" (*parakoloutheō*), meaning "to follow after; so to follow one as to be always at his side. To be always present, to attend one wherever he goes."[5] Jesus often criticized the people for always asking for a sign (Mt 12:38; Mk 8:11; Jn 4:48). Jesus warned of those who would come with false signs and wonders used to lead people astray (Mt 24:24; Mk 13:22; 2 Th 2:9; Rev 13:13; 16:14). Yet the disciples asked Jesus what signs to look for before his coming and he answered them in detail (Mt 24:3; Mk 13:4; Lk 21:7, 25). Jesus also performed many signs that caused people to believe in him (Jn 2:11, 23; 3:2; 6:2,14; 7:31; 9:16; 11:47; 12:18; 20:30; Acts 2:22,43; 4:30; 5:12; 6:8; 8:6, 13; 14:3; 15:12; Rm 15:19; 2 Cor 12:12; Heb 2:4).

Signs will accompany "those who have believed," meaning those who continue to believe.

5. Thayer, *Thayer's Greek-English Lexicon*, 387.

Study Guide	Notes
Question 19 ?	Casting out demons, speaking with new tongues, picking up snakes, drinking deadly poison, and laying hands on the sick for healing.
What signs are mentioned here specifically?	
Explanation ✓	Casting out demons is practiced by Jesus and his disciples throughout the book of Mark and the other Gospels.
	Speaking with new tongues is not mentioned until Pentecost (Acts 2), and is referred to as one of the gifts of the Spirit in 1 Cor 12:10; 14:2-19).
	While this is the only reference to picking up snakes in the Bible, Jesus' disciples tread on snakes and scorpions, and "over all the power of the enemy" (Lk 10:19).
	Mark's reference to drinking deadly poison only occurs here in the Bible. This suggests that Jesus' followers were subjected to poisoning, as they continue to be now in some countries.
	Jesus himself lays hands on the sick and heals them (Mt 9:18; Mk 6:5; 7:32; 8:23,25; Lk 4:40; 13:13), and commissions his disciples to heal the sick throughout the Gospels (Mt 10:1, 8; Mk 6:13; Lk 9:1; 10:9), healing being referred to as one of the gifts of the Spirit (1 Cor 12:9).
Question 20 ?	
Do you see a need for these kinds of signs today? Where and why?	

Study Guide	Notes

Read Mark 16:19

"So then, when the Lord Jesus had spoken to them, he was received up into heaven and sat down at the right hand of God. And they went out and preached everywhere, while the Lord worked with them, and confirmed the word by the signs that followed."

Question 21

Where did Jesus and the disciples go next?

Jesus was received into heaven and sat down at the right hand of God.

The disciples went out and preached everywhere

The Lord worked with them, confirming the word with signs.

10.

BEING JESUS' WITNESSES

LUKE 24:48-49 & ACTS 1:4-21

Study Guide	Notes
Background	Jesus tells his disciples that they must wait for the Spirit's empowerment in order to continue his mission in his physical absence. This continues to be true today.
Introduction	In all of the Gospels Jesus begins his ministry after he is first baptized. There at the Jordan River the Holy Spirit comes upon him, empowering him as God's beloved Son to announce the Kingdom of God.
	At the end of Luke's Gospel and the beginning of the Acts of the Apostles, the resurrected Jesus meets his disciples, sharing final words with them about their mission. He also tells them to wait in Jerusalem until they are empowered by the Spirit "from on high." In Acts 2 the Holy Spirit is poured out at Pentecost, empowering Jesus' disciples all present to advance the Kingdom of God as Jesus did.
Read Luke 24:48-49 📖	
"You are witnesses of <u>these things</u>. "And behold, I am sending forth the promise of my Father upon you; but you are to stay in the city until you are clothed with power from on high."	
Question 1 ?	
What does Jesus tell his disciples they are to do in these verses and what will Jesus do?	Jesus' disciples are witnesses of "these things."
	Jesus will send the promise of his Father upon them.
	They are to stay in the city until they are clothed with power from on high.

Study Guide	Notes
Explanation	A witness (*martus*) is "one who avers, or can aver, what he himself has seen or heard or knows by any other means." It can also mean "a person who has been deprived of life as the result of bearing witness to his beliefs — 'martyr.'"[1]
Question 2 What do "these things" refer to of which Jesus' followers are witnesses?	"These things" refer to the appearance of the resurrected Jesus to the eleven remaining disciples described in Luke 24:36-47.
Suggestion	Invite people to notice what comes immediately before Luke 4:48-49.
Read Luke 24:36-37 "While they were telling <u>these things</u>, he himself stood in their midst and said to them, "Peace be to you." But they were startled and frightened and thought that they were seeing a spirit.	
Question 3 What happens here and how do Jesus' disciples respond?	Two people, a man named Cleopas and his companion were telling the eleven disciples about how they had encountered the resurrected Jesus on the road to Emmaus (Luke 24:13-32) when Jesus stood in their midst. Jesus suddenly appeared said to them: "Peace be to you." The disciples were startled and frightened. They thought they were seeing a spirit.

1. Louw and Nida, *Greek-English Lexicon*, 20.67.

Study Guide	Notes

Question 4   ?

What are the "these things" referred to in Luke 24:36-37?

Cleopas and his companion were relating their conversation with the resurrected Jesus on the Road to Emmaus and how they finally recognized him.

Explanation ✓

The resurrected Jesus approached and began journeying with two disciples on the road to Emmaus. He asked them what they are discussing (Lk 24:13-17).

Cleopas responds: "Are you the only one visiting Jerusalem and unaware of the things which have happened here in these days?" And he said to them, "<u>What things</u>?"

They tell how they'd hoped Jesus was going to redeem Israel, but that the chief priests and rulers had given him the death sentence, and crucified him. Some women reported that an angel told them he's alive.

Jesus scolds them for not believing in all the prophets have spoken. "Was it not necessary for the Christ to suffer <u>these things</u> and to enter into his glory? (24:25-27).

"Beginning with Moses and with all the prophets, he explained to them the things concerning Himself in all the Scriptures.

When he stayed with them, he blessed and broke the bread; their eyes were opened and he disappeared.

Study Guide	Notes
	They returned to Jerusalem and told the eleven: "The Lord has really risen and has appeared to Simon." They began to relate their experiences on the road and how he was recognized by them in the breaking of the bread" (24:34-35).
Read Luke 24:38 📖	
"And he said to them, "Why are you troubled, and why do doubts arise in your hearts?"	
Question 5 ❓	
What did Jesus ask them and why?	"Why are you troubled? Why do doubts arise in your hearts?"
	Did Jesus want them to reflect on why they were troubled and doubting?
Question 6 ❓	
Would you be troubled and doubting if you were these disciples? If so, why?	
Read Luke 24:39-40 📖	
"See my hands and my feet, that it is I myself; touch me and see, for a spirit does not have flesh and bones as you see that I have." And when he had said this, he showed them his hands and his feet."	

Study Guide	Notes
Question 7 ?	
What does Jesus say and do next?	He tells them to see his hands and feet; that it's him.
	He invites them to touch him and see, stating that a spirit does not have flesh and bones like they can see that he has.
	He then shows them his hands and feet.
	Jesus wants his disciples to be assured that his physical body has come back to life.
Read Luke 24:41-43 📖	
"While they still could not believe it because of their joy and amazement, He said to them, "Have you anything here to eat?" They gave him a piece of a broiled fish; and he took it and ate it before them."	
Question 8 ?	
How did the disciples respond and what did Jesus do next?	They still could not believe it but they were joyful and amazed.
	Jesus asked them for something to eat.
	They gave him a piece of boiled fish.
	Jesus took the fish and ate it in front of them.
Question 9 ?	
Why are Jesus' actions here important?	He wants them and future followers to know that he had a resurrected body, and that he can still eat food as before.

Study Guide	Notes

Read Luke 24:44-45 📖

"Now he said to them, "These are my words which I spoke to you while I was still with you, that all things which are written about me in the Law of Moses and the Prophets and the Psalms must be fulfilled." Then he opened their minds to understand the Scriptures."

Question 10 ❓

What did Jesus say and do next?

He told his disciples they were seeing the fulfillment of what he had told them and what was written in the Old Testament Scriptures (the Law of Moses, the Prophets and the Psalms.

He then opened their minds to understand the Scriptures.

Question 11 ❓

Why is this important?

Jesus' life, death and resurrection fulfilled prophecies in the Old Testament, which is still sacred Scripture for disciples now.

We need revelation from God to understand the Scripture now, and the resurrected Jesus himself is our Teacher.

Read Luke 24:46-47 📖

"Thus it is written, that the Christ would suffer and rise again from the dead the third day, and that repentance for forgiveness of sins would be proclaimed in his name to all the nations, beginning from Jerusalem."

Study Guide	Notes

Question 12   ?

What does Jesus tell his disciples here in these final instructions?

That the Christ would suffer and rise from the dead on the third day.

That repentance for forgiveness of sins needed to be proclaimed in Jesus' name to all the nations, beginning there in Jerusalem.

Explanation   ✓

Jesus shares core teachings here, beginning with the clarification that the Christ, Israel's awaited Messiah liberator, would suffer, die and raise from the dead on the third day. On the road to Emmaus Jesus spoke in detail to two of his disciples about how Scripture (the law and prophets) announced that the Messiah would suffer (Jn 24:13-36).

Read Luke 24:48-49   📖

"You are witnesses of these things. "And behold, I am sending forth the promise of my Father upon you; but you are to stay in the city until you are clothed with power from on high."

Question 13   ?

What does Jesus tell his disciples here in these final instructions?

That they were to stay in the city until they are clothed with power from on high.

Study Guide	Notes

Explanation

As witnesses of Jesus' death and appearance to them after his resurrection, the disciples are commissioned to proclaim "repentance and forgiveness of sins" to all the nations, "in the name" of Jesus.

Proclaiming (*kērussō*) means "to be a herald; to officiate as herald; always with a suggestion of formality, gravity, and an authority which must be listened to and obeyed; to publish, proclaim openly: something which has been done."[2] John the Baptist modeled this kind of proclamation when he baptized, calling people to confess their sins, repent (change their way of thinking and behaving), and receive forgiveness. This was to be proclaimed "in Jesus' name" once Jesus ascended to heaven.

Jesus clearly stated that his disciples must wait in Jerusalem until he sent the "promise of the Father" upon them. Only after receiving this promise would they be "clothed with power from on high." The disciples were given "power and authority" directly from Jesus in Luke 9:1, "over all demons and to heal diseases." Receiving this power from heaven appears to be essential for continuing the Jesus' movement.

Read Acts 1:4-5

"Gathering them together, he commanded them not to leave Jerusalem, but to wait for what the Father had promised, "which," he said, "you heard of from me; for John baptized with water, but you will be baptized with the Holy Spirit not many days from now."

2. Thayer, *Thayer's Greek-English Lexicon*, 2784.

Study Guide	Notes

Question 14

What did Jesus do and say to his disciples here?

He gathered together his disciples and commanded them not to leave Jerusalem. He told them to "wait for what the Father had promised."

Jesus clarified that while John baptized with water they would soon be baptized with the Holy Spirit.

Explanation

Jesus' teaching here appears to clarify that John's baptism, which in his case included the Holy Spirit coming upon him and the Father declaring his beloved Son status, was to be followed by a distinct baptism with the Holy Spirit.

Jesus' earlier statement that "the promise of the Father" would come upon them and they would be baptized "with" or "in" the Holy Spirit, prepares us for what happens next at Pentecost.

Read Acts 2:1-4

"When the day of Pentecost had come, they were all together in one place. And suddenly there came from heaven a noise like a violent rushing wind, and it filled the whole house where they were sitting. And there appeared to them tongues as of fire distributing themselves, and they rested on each one of them. And they were all filled with the Holy Spirit and began to speak with other tongues, as the Spirit was giving them utterance."

Study Guide	Notes

Question 15   ?

What happened on the day of Pentecost according to these verses?

Jesus' disciples were gathered together when suddenly a violent rushing wind filled the house, and they were all filled with the Holy Spirit.

A tongue of fire rested on each person as the Spirit permitted.

Read Acts 2:5-13 📖

"Now there were Jews living in Jerusalem, devout men from every nation under heaven. And when this sound occurred, the crowd came together, and were bewildered because each one of them was hearing them speak in his own language. They were amazed and astonished, saying, "Why, are not all these who are speaking Galileans? "And how is it that we each hear them in our own language to which we were born? "Parthians and Medes and Elamites, and residents of Mesopotamia, Judea and Cappadocia, Pontus and Asia, Phrygia and Pamphylia, Egypt and the districts of Libya around Cyrene, and visitors from Rome, both Jews and proselytes, Cretans and Arabs — we hear them in our own tongues speaking of the mighty deeds of God. And they all continued in amazement and great perplexity, saying to one another, "What does this mean?" But others were mocking and saying, "They are full of sweet wine.""

Study Guide	Notes
Question 16 ?	
What happened next and how did people respond?	Jews living in Jerusalem from every nation in the world came together bewildered.
	Each person was amazed and astonished to hear simple Galileans speaking in their own foreign language.
	They asked how could it be that each of them were hearing them in their own birth language.
	They heard them in their own tongues speaking of the mighty deeds of God.
	Some people thought they were drunk.
Explanation ✓	The Holy Spirit manifested as a violent rushing wind and tongues of fire enabled the disciples to bear witness to Jesus in other languages, which people from other nations could understand. The Holy Spirit made it possible for humble, uneducated Galileans to communicate across huge language and cultural divides.

Study Guide	Notes

Read Acts 2:14-21 📖

But Peter, taking his stand with the eleven, raised his voice and declared to them: "Men of Judea and all you who live in Jerusalem, let this be known to you and give heed to my words. "For these men are not drunk, as you suppose, for it is only the third hour of the day; but this is what was spoken of through the prophet Joel:

'And it shall be in the last days,' God says, 'that I will pour forth of my Spirit on all mankind; and your sons and your daughters shall prophesy, and your young men shall see visions, and your old men shall dream dreams; even on my bondslaves, both men and women, I will in those days pour forth my Spirit and they shall prophesy. 'And I will grant wonders in the sky above and signs on the earth below, blood, and fire, and vapor of smoke. 'The sun will be turned into darkness and the moon into blood, before the great and glorious day of the Lord shall come. 'And it shall be that everyone who calls on the name of the Lord will be saved.'"

Study Guide	Notes
Question 17 ?	
How does Peter interpret the disciples speaking in foreign languages?	He tells the onlookers that the people speaking in tongues are not drunk.
	Rather, Old Testament prophecies (from Joel 2:28-32) are being fulfilled, that the Spirit would be poured out on all humankind.
	The Spirit enables their sons and daughters to prophesy.
	Old men will see visions, young men will dream dreams.
	The Spirit would even be poured out onto male and female slaves, who would prophesy.
	God will cause there to be dramatic wonders in the sky and signs on the earth before the "day of the Lord."
	Everyone who calls on the name of the Lord will be saved.
Question 18 ?	
According to all these Scriptures, what enables Jesus' disciples to bear witness?	The disciples were told by Jesus to "stay in the city until you are clothed with power from on high" (Lk 24:49).
	Then in Acts 1:8 Jesus said: "you will receive power when the Holy Spirit has come upon you; and you shall be my witnesses."
	Finally on the day of Pentecost the Holy Spirit filled the gathered believers, empowering them to speak in other languages. They prophesied in ways where the mighty deeds of God could be understood across all the barriers that separate people (language, nation, culture, age, gender, and social class).

Study Guide	Notes
Invitation ⟶	Close with a time of prayer, inviting the Holy Spirit to empower people to bear witness. Consider praying for the gift of prophesy to be released, as well as dreams, visions and the capacity to share the good news with people across all the lines that divide us.

11.

HEALING AND INCLUSION AT THE BEAUTIFUL GATE

ACTS 3:1-4:4

Study Guide	Notes
Background	Acts 3 describes the first healing story in Jesus' physical absence since his ascension. Just before this story in Acts 2, the Holy Spirit was poured out on the gathered believers, manifesting with a tongue of fire resting on each person and them speaking in different languages—empowering them to bear witness. Peter's preaching on the day of Pentecost led to 3,000 people coming to believe. Following this the gathered believers are presented... Peter and John were two of Jesus' disciples often mentioned as being present at key moments in the Gospels (Lk 5:1-11; 8:49-56; 9:28-43; 22:8-13).
Introduction	Peter and John are traveling together from their gathered community to the Temple on their way to participate in afternoon/evening prayers.
	In this first healing story after Pentecost numerous features of ministry combine, presenting a holistic approach that bridged divergent emphases.[1] These features will be written in the right-hand columns across from the verses where they appear.
	• Two-by-two ministry focusing on the excluded poor • The excluded take the initiative in transformation • Presence, personal connection and relationship • Prophetic seeing • Faith

---

1. See Bob Ekblad, *The Beautiful Gate: Enter Jesus' Global Liberation Movement.* Burlington: The People's Seminary Press, 2017.

Study Guide	Notes
	• Ministry of the word without money—only Jesus • Hands-on help, authority and divine healing • The power of God that empowers • Gathering and inclusion • Humble deflecting of credit away from self • Social prophetic exposure and critique • The name of Jesus • Grace and forgiveness freely-given • The theology of the cross • Repentance and conversion • The return of Jesus and the end of history • Prophesy fulfilled • Recruitment for mission to the world • Persecution
Suggestion	This Bible study can be done as one longer study (Acts 3:1-26 or two shorter studies, Acts 3:1-16 and 3:17-4:4.
Read Acts 3:1-2 📖	
"Now Peter and John were going up to the temple at the ninth hour, the hour of prayer. And a man who had been lame from his mother's womb was being carried along, whom they used to set down every day at the gate of the temple which is called Beautiful, in order to beg alms of those who were entering the temple."	**Two-by-two ministry focusing on the excluded poor.**

Study Guide	Notes
Question 1 ?	
Who are the characters in these verses, where are they and what are they doing?	Peter and John are going to pray in the temple at the hour of prayer. They encounter a man lame from birth who was being carried to sit outside the gate of the temple called "Beautiful" to beg for money from those going inside.
Question 2 ?	
Where do you encounter excluded people like the man lame from birth today?	
Explanation ✓	In Luke 10:1 Jesus appointed and sent out 70 disciples two-by-two, as laborers into the harvest to all the places where he was about to go. He gave them precise instructions: "Carry no money belt, no bag, no shoes; and greet no one on the way" (10:4). He told them to stay with those who welcomed them, to receive their hospitality and pray for their healing, announcing the Kingdom of God has come close to you (10:5-9). Here is the first time after Jesus has ascended to heaven and the Holy Spirit has been poured out at Pentecost that disciples are going out in pairs.
Read Acts 3:3 📖	
"When he saw Peter and John about to go into the temple, he began asking to receive alms."	**The excluded take the initiative in transformation**

Study Guide	Notes
Question 3 ?	The lame man sees Peter and John about to enter the temple and he asks them for alms.
What happens next?	
Explanation ✓	The Greek language used here is the language of spiritual seeing and prayer. The underlying Greek word for "see," *horao*, means physical seeing that is also spiritual (Lk 1:11, 22; 2:15, 17, 20, 26, 30;9:31, 36; 10:24; 21:27; 23:47; 24:34,39). "Asking," *erotao*, happens in the Gospels when people are asking Jesus to heal someone (Mk 7:26; Lk 4:38; 7:3; 9:2; 9:2; Acts 1:6), explain something (Mt 19:17; Mk 4:10); eat or stay with people (Lk 7:36; 11:37; Jn 4:40) or ask the Father for something in Jesus' name (Jn 4:47; 16:23, 26).
	The word "alms" (*eleēmosynē*) and not "money" is used here, a religious term meaning "that which is given to help the needy — 'gift, money given to the needy, charity donation.'"² The man is asking for help that those entering the Jewish temple would have considered a religious requirement.
Question 4 ?	
Where do people like the man lame from birth see and encounter religious people about to enter churches or other religious places?	

---

2. Louw and Nida, *Greek-English Lexicon*, 57.112.

Study Guide	Notes

Suggestion   !   Another possible question could be:

If you saw vulnerable "lame-from-birth" people's "seeing" or approaching you as invitations to experience God's Kingdom through relationship leading to miraculous healing, how would that change how you approach them?

Read Acts 3:4   📖

"But Peter, along with John, fixed his gaze on him and said, "Look at us!""

Presence, personal connection, and relationship

Question 5   ?

What do Peter and John do and say? Why do you think they say what they say?

They look at him intently and ask him to look at them. Their request that he look at them could show they are not ignoring him but moving closer towards him relationally.

Explanation   ✓

Prophetic seeing

The Greek word underlying "fix his gaze," *atenizo,* means to fix one's eyes attentively. It often involves prophetic seeing something God is showing someone (Lk 4:20; Acts 1:10; 3:12).

When Peter tells the lame man: "look at us!" the Greek verb meaning physical seeing, *blepo,* is used. This suggests Peter and John want to connect with the man personally as fellow humans.

Read Acts 3:5   📖

"And he began to give them his attention, expecting to receive something from them."

Faith

Study Guide	Notes
Question 6 ?	He looks at them expecting to receive something.
How does the lame man respond?	
Explanation ✓	Readers often assume the lame man was looking with expectation the Peter and John would give him money. However, the text doesn't say money or alms, but "something," a challenge our negative expectations (prejudice) towards beggars.
	The underlying Greek word translated "expecting to receive," *epechō*, means "to attend to, give attention to,"[3] or "to notice."[4]
Read Acts 3:6 📖	
"But Peter said, "I do not possess silver and gold, but what I do have I give to you: In the name of Jesus Christ the Nazarene — walk!"	**Ministry of the word without money—only Jesus**
Question 7 ?	Peter tells the lame man that he does not possess silver or gold. Instead, he offers to give him what he "has."
What does Peter say in response to the man lame from birth?	
	Peter then says to him: "In the name of Jesus Christ the Nazarene—walk!"

---

3. Thayer, *Thayer's Greek-English Lexicon*, 1907, Phil 2:7; 1 Tim 4:16.
4. Louw & Nida, *Greek-English Lexicon*, 24.33. See Luke 14:7.

Study Guide	Notes
Explanation ✓	Peter states that he does not have silver or gold, which is in alignment with the instructions Jesus gave his disciples and missionaries to go out as vulnerable guests (see Luke 9:3 and 10:4).
	Peter orders the man lame from birth to walk. He specifies in whose name he give the order: "In the name of Jesus Christ the Nazarene."
Question 8 ?	
What would it look like for us go out without money or other resources on missions today?	
Read Acts 3:7 📖	
"And seizing him by the right hand, he raised him up; and immediately his feet and his ankles were strengthened."	**Hands-on help, authority and healing**
Question 9 ?	
What did Peter do and what happened?	He seized him by the right hand and raised him up.
	Immediately his feet and ankles were strengthened.

Study Guide	Notes

Explanation

The verb "seize," *piazo* in Greek can mean to officially arrest, apprehend, capture, lay hands on,[5] and also includes the action of catching fish (Jn 21:3, 10).

In the Bible the right hand refers to God's intervention in the world. God's right hand upholds the psalmist (Ps 18:35) and is associated with saving strength (Ps 20:6; 60:5; 98:1; 108:6; 109:31; 110:5), and favor (Ps 44:3). "Nevertheless I am continually with you; you have taken hold of my right hand" (Ps 73:23). Gods right hand is associated with empowering his agents: "Let your hand be upon the man of your right hand, upon the son of man whom you made strong for yourself" (Ps 80:17). In the New Testament believers are raised in Christ to occupy the place at the Father's right hand, the source of spiritual authority (Eph 1:18-23; 2:6; Col 3:1).

Raise up comes from the Greek verb *egeiro*, which can mean to resurrect from the dead.[6]

Question 10

Who strengthened the man's feet and ankles?

There is no mention of who strengthened the man's feet and ankles. This is an example of what's called "the Divine passive," where God is the unnamed actor.

Later Peter proclaims that it was the name of Jesus that brought about the healing.

---

5. John 7:30, 32, 44; 8:20; 10:39; 11:57; Acts 12:4; 2 Cor 11:32; Rm 19:20.
6. Luke 7;14, 16, 22; 8:54; 9:7, 22; 20:37; 24:6, 34; Acts 3:15; 10:40; 13:30, 37; 26:8.

Study Guide	Notes
Read Acts 3:8 📖	
"With a leap he stood upright and began to walk; and he entered the temple with them, walking and leaping and praising God."	**The Power of God that empowers**
Question 11 ?	
What happened next and how did things change for the man?	The man lame from birth 1) leaps, 2) stands up straight, 3) begins to walk, 4) enters the temple with them, 5) walking, 6) leaping, and 7) praising God.
Read Acts 3:9-11 📖	
"And all the people saw him walking and praising God; and they were taking note of him as being the one who used to sit at the Beautiful Gate of the temple to beg alms, and they were filled with wonder and amazement at what had happened to him. While he was cling-ing to Peter and John, all the people ran together to them at the so-called portico of Solomon, full of amazement."	**Gathering and inclusion**
Question 12 ?	
How did the people inside the temple respond to the miracle?	All the people saw the man they knew as previously lame from birth walking and praising God.
	They were filled with wonder and amazement.
	While the lame man now healed clung to Peter and John everyone ran together, full of amazement.

Study Guide	Notes
Read Acts 3:12 📖	
"But when Peter saw this, he replied to the people, "Men of Israel, why are you amazed at this, or why do you gaze at us, as if by our own power or piety we had made him walk?	**Humble deflecting of credit away from self**
Question 13 ?	
How did Peter respond to the response?	He asked the people why they were so amazed, as if they had made them man walk through their own power or piety.
Read Acts 3:13-15 📖	
"The God of Abraham, Isaac and Jacob, the God of our fathers, has glorified his servant Jesus, the one whom you delivered and disowned in the presence of Pilate, when he had decided to release him. "But you disowned the Holy and Righteous One and asked for a murderer to be granted to you, but put to death the Prince of Life, the one whom God raised from the dead, a fact to which we are witnesses.	**Social prophetic exposure and critique**

Study Guide	Notes

Question 14   ?

What does Peter say to the people?

Peter evokes the God of his and the people's fathers, Abraham, Isaac, and Jacob.

He tells the people that their God glorified Jesus, who they delivered and denied Jesus before the Roman governor Pilate—even after he wanted to release him.

He exposes and denounces their disowning of the Holy and Righteous One, Jesus, and their asking for Barabbas (a murderer) in his place.

He confronts them with their crime of executing the Prince of Life, who God raised from the dead.

He states that he and his fellow disciples are witnesses to this.

Read Acts 3:16   📖

"And on the basis of faith in his name, it is the name of Jesus which has strengthened this man whom you see and know; and the faith which comes through him has given him this perfect health in the presence of you all."

The name of Jesus

Question 15   ?

According to Peter, how was the man lame from birth healed?

By faith in the name of Jesus

Study Guide	Notes
Explanation	Through out the New Testament followers of Jesus are told to make requests to God (Jn 14:13-14; 16:23), heal the sick (Acts 4:10; Jam 5:14), cast out demons (Mt 7:22; Mk 9:38; Lk 10:17; Acts 16:19) and exercise their spiritual authority in all things (Col 3:17) "in the name of Jesus." Making requests to God, healing, casting out demons and other actions.
Question 16 What chronic problems keep people excluded today? How might you address these conditions in the name of Jesus?	
Suggestion **and** **Invitation** ⟶	If you choose to end your study of Acts 3 here, looking at Acts 3:17-4:4 separately, consider ending with a time of prayer for people in the group with chronic physical or mental health issues.
Read Acts 3:17-18 "And now, brethren, I know that you acted in ignorance, just as your rulers did also. But the things which God announced beforehand by the mouth of all the prophets, that his Christ would suffer, he has thus fulfilled."	**Grace and forgiveness freely-given, and the theology of the cross**
Question 17 How does Peter explain things and what does that tell us about how God views the situation?	Peter calls the people his "brothers" (and sisters). He expresses confidence that they and their rulers acted in ignorance. He stated that the prophets had prophesied that God had announced that the Christ would suffer beforehand.

Study Guide	Notes
Explanation ✓	Peter's words here seem informed by Jesus' words on the cross: "Father, forgive them; for they do not know what they are doing" (Lk 23:34).
Read Acts 3:19 📖 "Therefore repent and return, so that your sins may be wiped away, in order that times of refreshing may come from the presence of the Lord."	**Repentance & conversion**
Question 18 ❓ How did Peter call the people to respond? What does he say God will do?	He called them to repent and return, with the result that their sins would be forgiven and times of refreshing would come from God.
Explanation ✓	"Repent," *metanoeō*, literally means to have another mind, to think differently or change one's mind. It can also mean to be sorry for one's sins, as it is paired with sackcloth and ashes (Mt 11:21; Lk 10:13). "Return," *epistrephō*, means to turn, return, or come back (Lk 2:20; 8:55; Acts 15:36). In Acts "large numbers… believed and turned to the Lord" (Acts 11:21). Paul invites the Gentiles in Lystra to "turn to the living God" (Acts 14:15).
Read Acts 3:20-21 📖 "And that he may send Jesus, the Christ appointed for you, whom heaven must receive until the period of restoration of all things about which God spoke by the mouth of his holy prophets from ancient time."	**The return of Jesus and the end of history**

Study Guide	Notes
Question 19 ?	
What more will God do in response to people's repentance and returning?	God will send Jesus Christ in his second coming, when all things will be restored.
Read Acts 3:22-24 📖	
"Moses said, 'The Lord your God will raise up for you from your own people a prophet like me. You must listen to whatever he tells you. And it will be that every soul that does not heed that prophet shall be utterly destroyed from among the people.' And likewise, all the prophets who have spoken, from Samuel and his successors onward, also announced these days."	**Prophecy fulfilled**
Question 20 ?	
What did Moses say according to Peter?	That God will raise up a prophet like himself from the people.
	People must listen to everything this prophet says.
	Everyone who does not listen to this prophet from among the people will be destroyed.
	All the prophets since Samuel announced these days.

Study Guide	Notes

Explanation ✓

Moses' prophesy regarding God's sending a prophet like himself who people must listen to is found in Deuteronomy 15:18-19.

Being utterly destroyed from among the people" is certainly grave. This is a direct citation from the Septuagint of Leviticus 23:29, which refers to people being cut off or destroyed who do not humble themselves on the Day of Atonement, when the people's sins are confessed and atoned for through sacrifice and priestly intercession."[7]

Read Acts 3:25-26 📖

"You are the descendants of the prophets and of the covenant that God gave to your ancestors, saying to Abraham, 'And in your descendants all the families of the earth shall be blessed.' When God raised up his servant, he sent him first to you, to bless you by turning each of you from your wicked ways.'"

Recruitment for mission to the world

Question 21 ?

What does Peter say about his audience?

He identifies them as "sons of the prophets and of the covenant."

He says they are the "seed" of Abraham through who "all the families of the earth shall be blessed."

He says that God raised up his Servant Jesus for them (the Jewish people) first, to bless them by turning them from their wicked ways.

---

7. Bob Ekblad, *The Beautiful Gate: Enter Jesus' Global Liberation Movement*, Burlington: The People's Seminary Press, 2017, p. 141-142.

Study Guide	Notes

Explanation ✓

In Acts 3:25 Peter is referring to God's call and promise to Abraham in Genesis 12:1-4.

In Acts 3:26 Peter is identifying Jesus as the Servant of the Lord in Isaiah 40-55.

Read Acts 4:1-4 📖

"As they were speaking to the people, the priests and the captain of the temple guard and the Sadducees came up to them, being greatly disturbed because they were teaching the people and proclaiming in Jesus the resurrection from the dead. And they laid hands on them and put them in jail until the next day, for it was already evening. But many of those who had heard the message believed; and the number of the men came to be about five thousand."

Persecution

Question 22 ?

What happens as Peter and John are speaking to the people?

The religious authorities come, greatly disturbed that they are teaching and proclaiming in Jesus the resurrection of the dead.

They arrest Peter and John and put them in jail.

Question 23 ?

What is the final outcome of the story?

Many people come to believe the message, about 5,000 men.

Invitation ⟶

Consider how you feel personally challenged and called to respond? End with a time of prayer. Consider how you would like to commit yourself afresh to any aspect of following Jesus.

12.

PHILIP'S MISSION IN SAMARIA

ACTS 8:4-13, 25-40

Study Guide	Notes
Background	The early church is described as a vibrant community of people who ate, worshipped, received teaching and cared for people in need together (Acts 2:43-47; 5:42). When there are complaints from Greek-speaking Jewish widows about discrimination at their equivalent of a food bank, the apostles set criterion for choosing deacons
	Seven Greek men are chosen by the community to wait on Greek-speaking widows (Acts 6:3-4). Stephen, Philip, and four others were appointed, and the apostles laid hands on them (Acts 6:6). Stephen is then described as being "full of grace and power, and performing great wonders and signs among the people" (Acts 6:8), leading to false accusations of blasphemy (Acts 6:11-15). Stephen preaches a powerful sermon that challenges Jewish listeners, who stone him to death (Acts 7). After Stephen is martyred, a great persecution starts against followers of Jesus in the church of Jerusalem. Acts 8:1-3 describes Saul's campaign to arrest and imprison. Philip, the second deacon named in Acts 6:5 is then featured.
Introduction	Philip is among those who are scattered by the persecution, who then go about preaching the word. He went to a city of Samaria and began preaching as Jesus had, and continued to be guided by the Spirit.
Read Acts 8:4-5 📖	
"Therefore, those who had been scattered went about preaching the word. Philip went down to the city of Samaria and began proclaiming Christ to them."	

Study Guide	Notes
Question 1 ❓	
What happens due to the persecution against Jesus-followers? Where does Philip go and what does he do?	Everyone who is scattered goes about preaching the word.
	Philip went down to a Samaritan city and proclaims Christ to them.
Question 2 ❓	
Why did Philip go to a city of Samaria?	Everyone who is scattered goes about preaching the word.
	Philip went down to a Samaritan city and proclaims Christ to them.
Explanation ✓	Notice that no one sent Philip to Samaria. Rather he went there on his own accord, showing the freedom these early missionaries felt to carry on with Jesus' ministry.
	Philip may well have chosen to go to one of the cities of Samaria based on Jesus' example of ministering among the excluded Samaritans (Lk 17:11; Jn 4), and his words to the eleven in Acts 1:8. "And you shall be my witnesses both in Jerusalem, and in all Judea and Samaria, and even to the remotest part of the earth."
	The apostles had already been ministering in Jerusalem and Judea, which was now blocked due to persecution. Samaria was next on the list of Jesus' priorities. Jewish persecutors would likely not enter Samaria to avoid becoming "unclean." Nor would they see it as having any importance. This would make it an ideal refuge for fleeing Christians.
	Since the apostles had laid hands on Philip at the beginning of his ministry, the Spirit was upon him wherever he went.

Study Guide	Notes

Question 3   ?

What would be the equivalent of Samaria or Samaritans in your community?

Read Acts 8:6-8   📖

"The crowds with one accord were giving attention to what was said by Philip, as they heard and saw the signs which he was performing. For in the case of many who had unclean spirits, they were coming out of them shouting with a loud voice; and many who had been paralyzed and lame were healed. So there was much rejoicing in that city.

Question 4   ?

How do the people of Samaria respond to Philip and what happens there?

The crowds of Samaritans appear to unanimously pay attention to Philip's preaching, hearing and seeing signs he was performing.

Many people were being delivered of unclean spirits, shouting with loud voices.

Many who had been paralyzed and lame were healed.

There was a lot of rejoicing in that Samaritan city.

Explanation   ✓

This description of Philip's mission in Samaria is followed by a story of Simon, a man who practiced magic arts and had a big following. When he saw Philip preaching the good news of the Kingdom of God and the name of Jesus, baptizing people and performing miracles, he too believes and is amazed (Acts 8:9-13).

Study Guide	Notes

The apostles send Peter and John, who lay hands on the new Samaritan believers, who receive the Holy Spirit (8:14-17). When Simon tries to give the apostles money for the power to lay hands on people as they do, Peter confronts him and he repents (8:20-24). They then head back to Jerusalem, preaching the gospel to other Samaritan villages. This sets the stage for God's next assignment for Philip.

Read Acts 8:26 📖

"But an angel of the Lord spoke to Philip saying, "Get up and go south to the road that descends from Jerusalem to Gaza." (This is a desert road.)"

Question 5 ?

What happens here?

An angel of the Lord speaks to Philip, telling him to get up and go south to a specific desert road going from Jerusalem to Gaza.

Explanation ✓

The word used for the angel of the Lord's speaking to Philip, *laleo*, is the most common and humble term for speaking, such as "say." Elsewhere in Luke and Acts the angel of the Lord is described as appearing.

The angel gives two commands, "get up!" and "go!", offering a specific destination but no further instructions.

Going back towards Jerusalem would have brought Philip back to where Saul was persecuting believers.

Study Guide	Notes

Question 6

What would be an example of an equivalent desert road in your setting?

Question 7

How would you respond if you sensed you were being told by an angel to go to a remote place without any further instructions.

Read Acts 8:27-28

"So he got up and went; and there was an Ethiopian eunuch, a court official of Candace, queen of the Ethiopians, who was in charge of all her treasure; and he had come to Jerusalem to worship, and he was returning and sitting in his chariot, and was reading the prophet Isaiah."

Question 8

What did Philip do and what did he find?

Philip got up and went, and there at the destination was an Ethiopian eunuch, treasurer of the queen sitting in his chariot reading the prophet Isaiah.

Explanation

We do not know from this description whether the Ethiopian eunuch was Jewish. We do know that he was returning to his country after having come to Jerusalem to worship, and that he was reading one of the prophetic books of the Jewish Scriptures—Isaiah.

Study Guide	Notes

Background

A eunuch is "a castrated male person," or human male who without being castrated is by nature incapable of sexual intercourse — 'impotent male.'"[1] Eunuch's were considered unclean and were shunned in the first century. See the following quotes:

"Shun eunuchs and flee all dealings with those who have deprived them-selves of their virility and of those fruits of generation, which God has given to men for the increase of our race; expel them even as infanticides who withal have destroyed the means of procreation."[2] Josephus, 37 CE – c. 100 CE.

"Eunuchs are men who belie their sex and are affected with effemination, who debase the currency of nature and violate it by assuming the passions and the outward form of licentious women."[3] Philo of Alexandria

"A eunuch was neither man, nor woman, but something composite, hybrid and monstrous, alien to human nature."[4] Lucian of Samosata, 125 CE – c.180 CE

Read Acts 8:29 📖

"Then the Spirit said to Philip, "Go up and join this chariot."

---

1. Louw and Nida, *Greek-English Lexicon*, 9.25, 9.28.

2. Josephus, *Jewish Antiquities*, 4.292(4.8.40.

3. Philo of Alexandria, De Specialibus Legibus, 1.324-25.

4. Lucian of Samosata, *Eunuchus*, in *Lucian, Volume 5*, Translated by Harmon, A. M London: W. Heinemann Macmillan, 1936, 329-345.

Study Guide	Notes
Question 9 ?	"Go up and join this chariot."
What did the Spirit say to Philip? What does this tell us about how God views the Ethiopian eunuch?	The Spirit cares about the eunuch. God does not discriminate against the eunuch, but recruits Philip to pursue him.
Explanation ✓	In Matthew 19:12 Jesus himself expressed acceptance of eunuchs, regardless of the reasons for their condition. "For there are eunuchs who were born that way from their mother's womb; and there are eunuchs who were made eunuchs by men; and there are also eunuchs who made themselves eunuchs for the sake of the Kingdom of Heaven. He who is able to accept this, let him accept it."
Read Acts 8:30 📖	
"Philip ran up and heard him reading Isaiah the prophet, and said, "Do you understand what you are reading?	
Question 10 ?	Philip 1) ran up, 2) heard him reading Isaiah and 3) asked him: "Do you understand what you are reading?"
What did Philip do? How did it differ from what the Spirit said?	The Spirit only told him to go up and join the chariot.

Study Guide	Notes

Explanation ✓

The Spirit, like the angel of the Lord, only gives two commands, without any explanation. This is the last time God speaks in this story.

Philip's question "Do you understand what you are reading?" may be understandable if we consider that the eunuch was reading the Jewish Scriptures. He was likely reading in Greek and not Hebrew, as it is the Greek version of Isaiah that is cited in Acts 8:32-33 (see explanation below).

Question 11 ?

What do Philip's words and actions tell us about the kind of person he is?

Philip acts in obedience to the Spirit, but also takes his own initiative, asking a question that he was not told to ask that shows he cares that the Ethiopian eunuch understands what he's reading in the Bible.

Read Acts 8:31 📖

"And he said, "Well, how could I, unless someone guides me?" And he invited Philip to come up and sit with him."

Question 12 ?

How does the Ethiopian eunuch court official respond?

The eunuch responds humbly: "Well, how could I, unless someone guides me?"

He then invites Philip to come up and sit with him.

Explanation ✓

The Greek term used here for the Spirit guiding, *hodegeo*, reminds of the reader of the Holy Spirit's action of "guiding" to all truth (Jn 16:13).

Study Guide	Notes

Read Acts 8:32-33 📖

"Now the passage of Scripture which he was reading was this: "He was led as a sheep to slaughter; and as a lamb before its shearer is silent, so he does not open his mouth. In humiliation his judgment was taken away; who will relate his generation? For his life is removed from the earth.""

Question 13 ?

What Scripture is the Ethiopian eunuch reading and why do you think he might he have questions about it?

Isaiah 53:7-8

Explanation ✓

Acts 8:32-33 cites directly from the Greek Version of Isaiah 53:7-8 (Septuagint). The Septuagint version of Isaiah 53:8 emphasizes that through the Servant's humiliation, judgement is taken away, and asks the question "who will tell his generation? since his life is removed from the earth." This makes the text relatable to the eunuch. In contrast the English translation of the Hebrew text of Isaiah 53:8 reads: "By oppression and judgment he was taken away; and as for his generation, who considered that he was cut off out of the land of the living.

Read Acts 8:34 📖

"The eunuch answered Philip and said, "Please tell me, of whom does the prophet say this? Of himself or of someone else?"

Study Guide	Notes
Question 14　　　　　　?	He may have identified his own castration with the servant's being lead as a lamb to the slaughter.
Why might this Scripture be relevant to the eunuch?	
	Being castrated, who could not have children, he could identify with the servant who did not have a generation.
Explanation　　✓	It is interesting that the man is referred to here not as the Ethiopian but as the eunuch. In fact that he is Ethiopian is only mentioned once (Acts 8:27), whereas that he is a eunuch is mentioned five times (Acts 8:27,34,36,38,39).
	Since the Ethiopian was court official of Candace, the queen of Ethiopia, in charge of her treasure, he may have been forcibly castrated, which is supported by his identification with Isaiah 53:7's "as a sheep to the slaughter, and "as a lamb before its shearer is silent."[5]

5. "Eunuchs in the ancient world were victims of violence, sexual exploitation, and social condemnation. Castration is violating; it assaults masculinity. Ancient Greek or Latin speakers had various words to differentiate whether a male's testicles had been crushed or pounded, torn from the body or cut out of it. This was often done to degrade men who had been conquered in war. 2 Kings 20:18 and Isaiah 39:7 recount how King Hezekiah's sons were captured, castrated and enslaved. The intent was to humiliate a weak Israelite king and establish Babylonian dominance. The sexual exploitation of eunuchs is widely depicted in the ancient literature. Powerful men used eunuchs for their sexual gratification. Aristocratic women would sometimes wait until **after puberty** to have a male slave castrated "so they could be sexually useful without worry about pregnancy." Alternatively, boy victims of pederasty were often castrated **prior to puberty** in order to preserve their desirability. Rather than being asexual or celibate, eunuchs were often sex slaves." Eric Mason, "What is a Biblical approach to the transgender community? Why should Christians work with the transsexuals?"in Glenn Miles and Christa Foster Crawford, eds., *Stopping the Traffick:A Christian Response to Sexual Exploitation and Trafficking*, Oxford: Regnum, 2014.

Study Guide	Notes

Read Acts 8:35 📖

"Then Philip opened his mouth, and beginning from this Scripture he preached Jesus to him."

Question 15 ?

What did Philip do next?

Philip began speaking, proclaiming Jesus to him.

Explanation ✓

Opening one's mouth associates what Philip is about to say with prophetic utterance (See Ps 81:10; Jr 1:9; Ez 3:1; Mt 5:1).

Philip literally "announced Jesus" to him. The Greek verb *euaggelizō* is used here, meaning "to announce good news ("evangelize") especially the gospel: — declare, bring (declare, show) glad (good) tidings, preach (the gospel).[6] Yet the content of the good news is Jesus himself.

Isaiah 53:7-8 is about the Servant of the Lord in Isaiah's posture of surrender, which is seen as being fulfilled by Jesus.

Read Acts 8:36 📖

"As they went along the road they came to some water; and the eunuch said, "Look! Water! What prevents me from being baptized?"

Question 16 ?

How did the Ethiopian respond to Philip's sharing?

When the chariot came to some water the eunuch draws Philip's attention to it. He asks him if there's anything that would keep him from being able to be baptized then and there.

6. Key Dictionary of Greek New Testament, 2097.

Study Guide	Notes

Read Acts 8:37a 📖

"And Philip said, "If you believe with all your heart, you may.""

Question 17 ?

How does Philip respond to the eunuch's request?

He asks the eunuch whether he believes with his whole heart?

Explanation ✓

Philip does not clarify what he thinks the eunuch needs to believe in order to be baptized. He appears to make it easy for the eunuch, though he does emphasize the important of whole-hearted belief.

Read Acts 8:37b-38 📖

"And he answered and said, "I believe that Jesus Christ is the Son of God." And he ordered the chariot to stop; and they both went down into the water, Philip as well as the eunuch, and he baptized him.""

Question 18 ?

How did the man respond and what then did Philip do?

The man confessed that he believed that Jesus Christ is the Son of God.

It is difficult to know whether Philip or the eunuch ordered the chariot to stop.

Both Philip and the eunuch went down into the water together and Philip baptized him.

Study Guide	Notes

Explanation

The eunuch's affirmation of Jesus' identity as Christ (Messiah) and "Son of God" was not presented to him by Philip, and is only possible through revelation. When Jesus asks his disciples who people say he is in Matthew 16:15-17, Peter responds: "You are the Christ, the Son of the living God." Jesus then said to him: "Blessed are you, Simon Barjona, because flesh and blood did not reveal this to you, but my Father who is in heaven."

Read Acts 8:39-40

"When they came up out of the water, the Spirit of the Lord snatched Philip away; and the eunuch no longer saw him, but went on his way rejoicing. But Philip found himself at Azotus, and as he passed through he kept preaching the gospel to all the cities until he came to Caesarea. "

Question 19

What happened the Philip and Ethiopian eunuch next?

The Spirit of the Lord snatched Philip away. The eunuch didn't see him again but continued his journey rejoicing.

Philip "found himself" in Azotus, from where he traveled until he arrived in Caesarea, preaching the gospel to all the cities he passed through.

Study Guide	Notes

Question 20

What does this story tell us about God and about being led by the Spirit in ministry?

God sends his people on precise missions. Once the mission is accomplished the Spirit moves them on to new assignments.

God knows who is seeking truth and open to hosting a messenger.

God sends messengers to bring good news to people of other nations, in this case Ethiopia.

God pursues people like this eunuch, who might normally be excluded by society due to their condition.

God works through people to bring good news to those who have not heard the liberating message.

Philip is not told what to do when he finds himself in Azotus. He decides for himself what to do, in alignment with Jesus' example and teachings in the Gospels.

Study Guide	Notes
Explanation ✓	Being guided by Spirit is about responding to people's actual questions. Philip gives the eunuch agency and respect.
	The Ethiopian eunuch takes initiative—provoking Philip's response "in the Spirit."
	Philip says, "If you believe with all your heart, you may." And the eunuch answered and said, "I believe that Jesus Christ is the Son of God" (Acts 8:37).
	The eunuch confesses something the Spirit gives him to confess: Nobody can say Jesus Christ is Lord except by the Spirit (Mt 16:15-17).
	Being led by the Spirit means:
	• Practicing the teachings of Jesus known from the Gospel accounts • Responding to God's voice • Paying attention to circumstances • Listening to the Spirit • Responding to the Spirit's precise direction • Listening to people • Asking the right questions • Answering people's questions "in the Spirit" to interpret Scripture • Responding to people's requests • Inviting people to affirm their faith • Getting into the water with them (baptism) • Surrendering yourself for the next mission
Invitation ⟶	Invite people to consider surrendering to the Holy Spirit, giving God permission to recruit them to engage more fully in Jesus' ministry.

13.

PETER'S CALL AND PROCLAMATION TO EXCLUDED OUTSIDERS

ACTS 10:1-48

Study Guide	Notes
Background	Peter's call to reach to non-Jewish people begins with the story of the Roman centurion Cornelius in Acts 10. This story follow's Philip's preaching in Samaria and encounter with the Ethiopian eunuch in Acts 8, and the conversion of Saul, his encounter with Ananias, and the beginning of Paul's ministry in Acts 9:1-31. Peter is then featured in two miracle stories, the healing of a paralytic named Aeneas in Acts 9:32-35 and the resurrection of Tabitha in Joppa in Acts 9:36-43.
Introduction	Acts 10:1 begins with a description of Cornelius, a Roman centurion who lives in the port city of Caesarea, where there is also a Roman garrison. Peter is staying in Joppa, in a house by the sea, a day's walk South of Caesarea. There while praying on his roof he receives a call to visit Cornelius.
Read Acts 10:1-2	
"Now there was a man at Caesarea named Cornelius, a centurion of what was called the Italian cohort, a devout man and one who feared God with all his household, and gave many alms to the Jewish people and prayed to God continually."	
Question 1	
What do we know about Cornelius?	He was a Roman centurion of the Italian cohort.
	He was devout and feared God, together with his household, giving alms to the Jewish people and praying continually.

Study Guide	Notes

Question 2 ?

Who would be equivalents of Roman centurions today?

Read Acts 10:3-4 📖

"About the ninth hour of the day he clearly saw in a vision an angel of God who had just come in and said to him, "Cornelius!" And fixing his gaze on him and being much alarmed, he said, "What is it, Lord?" And he said to him, "Your prayers and alms have ascended as a memorial before God."

Question 3 ?

What happened to Cornelius? What do the angel's actions and words tell us about God?

He saw a vision of an angel coming in and calling his name "Cornelius!"

He fixed his gaze on him, really upset and said to the angel: "What is it Lord?"

The angel said that his prayers and alms had ascended as a memorial to God.

Study Guide	Notes

Explanation ✓

Cornelius sees "an angel of God," and not "the angel of the Lord." He sees the angel "in a vision." The term here for "vision," *horama*, is used in a precise way to describe a visual revelation, as when Jesus' select disciples see him transfigured before them (Mt 17:9), Moses' seeing the vision in the desert followed by the voice of the Lord (Acts 7:31), and the Lord speaking to Ananias in a vision to go an pray for Saul (Acts 9:10, 12). Paul sees a vision of a Macedonian man, inviting him to Macedonia (Acts 16:9-10), and again in Acts 18:9. It is significant that Cornelius, a Roman centurion is encountered much like Moses, the disciples and Paul.

Question 4 ?

What do the angel's actions and words tell us about God?

God takes the initiative, sending messengers to individuals who he knows by name.

God notices our actions and prayers and responds.

God does not discriminate, but personally manifests himself to people regardless of their religion, or their racial or national origin.

Read Acts 10:5-6 📖

"Now dispatch some men to Joppa and send for a man named Simon, who is also called Peter; he is staying with a tanner named Simon, whose house is by the sea."

Study Guide	Notes
Question 5 ?	
What does the angel tell Cornelius to do? Why?	He tells Cornelius to dispatch men to Joppa and send for a man named Simon.
	The angel gives a precise location of where to find Simon Peter: staying with a man named Simon, who is a tanner living by the sea.
Read Acts 10:7-8 📖	
"When the angel who was speaking to him had left, he summoned two of his servants and a devout soldier of those who were his personal attendants, and after he had explained everything to them, he sent them to Joppa."	
Question 6 ?	
What does Cornelius do?	He called for two of his servants and a devout soldier, and after explaining everything to them he sent them to Joppa.
Read Acts 10:9-10 📖	
"On the next day, as they were on their way and approaching the city, Peter went up on the housetop about the sixth hour to pray. But he became hungry and was desiring to eat; but while they were making preparations, he fell into a trance;"	
Question 7 ?	
What happens to Peter in these verses?	While the men were on their way to Joppa, Peter was on the top of his house praying. He became hungry and fell into a trance while they were preparing food.

Study Guide	Notes

Explanation ✓

The Greek word for trance (*ekstasis*), which is "a vision accompanied by an ecstatic psychological state — 'ecstatic vision,'[1] though it can also mean "a state of intense amazement, to the point of being beside oneself with astonishment — 'amazement, astonishment.'[2] See Acts 22:17.

Read Acts 10:11-13 📖

"and he saw the sky opened up, and an object like a great sheet coming down, lowered by four corners to the ground, and there were in it all kinds of four-footed animals and crawling creatures of the earth and birds of the air. A voice came to him, "Get up, Peter, kill and eat!"

Question 8 ?

What does Peter see in his vision?

The sky opened up and something like a sheet was being lowered down by its four corners, filled with all kinds of animals, crawling creatures and birds.

A voice came to him saying, "Get up, Peter, kill and eat!"

Explanation ✓

The four-footed animals, crawling creatures and birds are all "unclean" animals that religious Jews were prohibited from eating based on Old Testament law.

---

1. Louw and Nida, *Greek-English Lexicon*, 33.489.
2. Louw and Nida, *Greek-English Lexicon*, 25.217.

Study Guide	Notes
Question 9 ? While this would vary from culture to culture, what would be some equivalents of these "unclean," prohibited things for you today?	
Read Acts 10:14 📖 "But Peter said, "By no means, Lord, for I have never eaten anything unholy and unclean."	
Question 10 ? How does Peter respond to the voice?	Peter refused to obey the instructions, responding to the voice, who he identifies as "Lord." He then said he'd never eaten anything unholy and unclean.
Read Acts 10:15-16 📖 "Again a voice came to him a second time, "What God has cleansed, no longer consider unholy." This happened three times, and immediately the object was taken up into the sky."	
Question 11 ? How does God respond back to Peter?	A voice came a second time, telling Peter that what God has cleaned is no longer unholy. This happened three times.
Explanation ✓	Notice that the voice may not be God's voice, as it says: "What God has cleansed," and not "What I have cleansed."

Study Guide	Notes

Read Acts 10:17-18 📖

"Now while Peter was greatly perplexed in mind as to what the vision which he had seen might be, behold, the men who had been sent by Cornelius, having asked directions for Simon's house, appeared at the gate; and calling out, they were asking whether Simon, who was also called Peter, was staying there."

Question 12 ?

What happens next?

> While Peter is greatly perplexed about the vision, the men Cornelius had sent found Simon's house and showed up at his gate, asking if Peter was staying there.

Explanation ✓

> Peter is described as "greatly perplexed," which only occurs in extremely unusual circumstances, as when Herod hears of Jesus, thinking he must be John the Baptist risen from the dead (Lk 9:7). The onlookers at Pentecost are perplexed (Acts 2:12), as is the captain of the temple guard when he finds Peter has escaped prison (Acts 5:24).

Read Acts 10:19-20 📖

"While Peter was reflecting on the vision, the Spirit said to him, "Behold, three men are looking for you. "But get up, go downstairs and accompany them without misgivings, for I have sent them myself."

Question 13 ?

What happens next?

> While Peter was reflecting on the vision, the Spirit told him that three men were looking for him, and that he should go with them without question as they are went by God.

Study Guide	Notes

Read Acts 10:21-23

"Peter went down to the men and said, "Behold, I am the one you are looking for; what is the reason for which you have come?" They said, "Cornelius, a centurion, a righteous and God-fearing man well-spoken of by the entire nation of the Jews, was divinely directed by a holy angel to send for you to come to his house and hear a message from you." So he invited them in and gave them lodging."

Question 14

What did Peter do and what happened next?

Peter went down to the men, telling them he's the one they are looking for.

The men explain how Cornelius had been directed by an angel to send for Peter to come to his house.

Peter invited them in and let him stay in his house.

Question 15

How did Peter's actions differ from what the Spirit had instructed him.

Peter didn't go immediately with the men. He invited them into his house and gave them lodging.

Explanation

Peter does not accompany the men immediately, but first show's them hospitality. Peter's welcoming Gentile visitors into his home appears to result from interpreting the vision to partake of the unclean and unholy creatures.

Study Guide	Notes

Read Acts 10:24-27

"And on the next day he got up and went away with them, and some of the brethren from Joppa accompanied him. On the following day he entered Caesarea. Now Cornelius was waiting for them and had called together his relatives and close friends. When Peter entered, Cornelius met him, and fell at his feet and worshiped him. But Peter raised him up, saying, "Stand up; I too am just a man." As he talked with him, he entered and found many people assembled."

Question 16 ?

What does Peter do next and what happens?

On the next day Peter got up and went away with the men, as the Spirit had told him. Some fellow believers from Joppa went with him.

They came to Caesarea, where they found Cornelius waiting for them.

Cornelius fall at his feet and worshiped him when he came into his home.

Peter raised him up, told him to get up, insisting that he was a man just like Cornelius.

As he was talking with him he entered and found many people gathered.

Study Guide	Notes

Explanation

The Spirit had told Peter when he was in a trance: "Get up, go downstairs and accompany them without misgivings" (Acts 10:20), without saying anything about bringing along fellow believers with him. That some of the brothers from Joppa went with Peter shows both their freedom to not follow the Spirit's instructions exactly, and their solidarity with Peter in his accepting being summoned by a Roman centurion who was a Gentile.

Read Acts 10:28-29

"And he said to them, "You yourselves know how unlawful it is for a man who is a Jew to associate with a foreigner or to visit him; and yet God has shown me that I should not call any man unholy or unclean. That is why I came without even raising any objection when I was sent for. So I ask for what reason you have sent for me.""

Question 17

How does Peter introduce himself and his reason for coming?

He appeals to his audience's prior knowledge that is it unlawful for a Jew to associate with a foreigner or visit him.

He tells them that God had shown him he shouldn't call anyone unholy or unclean, and for that reason he came when he was called by them.

Study Guide	Notes
Question 18 ?	God does not see anyone as unholy or unclean.
What is God like according to Peter's introduction in these verses, and how might this impact his listeners.	This would put his listeners at ease, as otherwise they might be defensive or assume that God and Peter are judging them.
Question 19 ?	
What would be an equivalent situation today?	While this would vary from culture to culture, examples could include addressing a message that God doesn't see anyone as unholy or unclean to people you or most in society would exclude, such as someone in the category of: drug dealer, bounty hunter, sex-offender, sexual minority, organized crime leader, Jihadist extremist, White supremacist, national enemy combatant…
Read Acts 10:30-33	
"Cornelius said, "Four days ago to this hour, I was praying in my house during the ninth hour; and behold, a man stood before me in shining garments, and he said, 'Cornelius, your prayer has been heard and your alms have been remembered before God. 'Therefore send to Joppa and invite Simon, who is also called Peter, to come to you; he is staying at the house of Simon the tanner by the sea.' "So I sent for you immediately, and you have been kind enough to come. Now then, we are all here present before God to hear all that you have been commanded by the Lord to speak."	

Study Guide	Notes

Question 20

What does Cornelius recount to his guests?

Cornelius explains to Peter the details of the vision that caused him to send for him.

Read Acts 10:34-36

Opening his mouth, Peter said:

"I most certainly understand now that God is not one to show partiality, but in every nation the man who fears him and does what is right is welcome to him. The word which he sent to the sons of Israel, preaching peace through Jesus Christ (he is Lord of all)."

Explanation

Opening one's mouth associates what Peter is about to say with prophetic utterance (See Ps 81:10; Jr 1:9; Ez 3:1; Mt 5:1).

Question 21

What does Peter emphasize here and why?

God does not discriminate.

Anyone from any nation who fears (respects) God and does what is right is welcomed.

Peter emphasizes that the word God sent to the children of Israel was about preaching peace through Jesus Christ, who is Lord of all (and not the Lord of Jews).

Study Guide	Notes
Question 22 ?	Cornelius and his non-Jewish family and friends would have felt included, happy to hear God does not show preference.
How would this message impact Peter's non-Jewish audience?	They may have felt challenged or affirmed by the message that all who fear God and do what is right are welcome to him.

Read Acts 10:37-38 📖

"You yourselves know the thing which took place throughout all Judea, starting from Galilee, after the baptism which John proclaimed. You know of Jesus of Nazareth, how God anointed him with the Holy Spirit and with power, and how he went about doing good and healing all who were oppressed by the devil, for God was with him."

Question 23 ?	God anointed Jesus with the Holy Spirit and power.
What actions of Jesus does Peter emphasize here? What does this tell us about Jesus?	He went about doing good and healing all who were oppressed by the devil— for God was with him.

Study Guide	Notes

Acts 10:39-43

"We are witnesses of all the things he did both in the land of the Jews and in Jerusalem. They also put him to death by hanging him on a cross. God raised him up on the third day and granted that he become visible, not to all the people, but to witnesses who were chosen beforehand by God, that is, to us who ate and drank with him after he arose from the dead. And he ordered us to preach to the people, and solemnly to testify that this is the One who has been appointed by God as Judge of the living and the dead. Of him all the prophets bear witness that through his name everyone who believes in him receives forgiveness of sins."

Question 24   ?

What are the core teachings Peter emphasizes here?

Peter and the other disciples witnessed Jesus' actions firsthand, leading to him being executed.

God raised Jesus from the dead on the third day.

The resurrected Jesus appeared to many people.

God ordered Peter and the other apostles to preach to the people, and to testify that Jesus will judge the living and the dead.

The prophets testified that through Jesus' name there's forgiveness of sins for all those who believe in him.

Study Guide	Notes

Question 25

What kind of response to the message does Peter suggest at the end of his sermon?

Believing in Jesus and receiving forgiveness for sins.

Read Acts 10:44-46

"While Peter was still speaking these words, the Holy Spirit fell upon all those who were listening to the message. All the circumcised believers who came with Peter were amazed, because the gift of the Holy Spirit had been poured out on the Gentiles also. For they were hearing them speaking with tongues and exalting God."

Question 26

What happens as Peter is preaching?

The Holy Spirit fell on those who were listening to Peter's message.

All the Jews who came with Peter (the circumcised) were amazed that the gift of the Holy Spirit had been poured out on the non-Jews (Gentiles).

This was manifested by their speaking in tongues and worshipping God.

Read Acts 10:47-48

"Then Peter answered, 'Surely no one can refuse the water for these to be baptized who have received the Holy Spirit just as we did, can he?'And he ordered them to be baptized in the name of Jesus Christ. Then they asked him to stay on for a few days."

Study Guide	Notes
Question 27 ?	
How did Peter respond?	Peter insists that Cornelius and his household be baptized with water, since they've already been baptized by the Holy Spirit.
Question 28 ?	
What would it look like to practice Peter's radical openness in your setting? What most excited you and what do you find most difficult about this story?	
Invitation ——▶	Take time to pray together about how you feel personally challenged and inspired by this story? Consider giving God your permission to recruit you for similar missions.

www.ingramcontent.com/pod-product-compliance
Lightning Source LLC
Chambersburg PA
CBHW061154120626
46546CB00005B/2055